Practical Home Handbook

Sewing
Skills & Techniques

Practical Home Handbook
Sewing
Skills & Techniques

Dorothy Wood

LORENZ BOOKS

This edition published by
Lorenz Books in 2002

© Anness Publishing Limited 2000, 2002

Lorenz Books is an imprint of
Anness Publishing Limited
Hermes House
88–89 Blackfriars Road
London SE1 8HA

Published in the USA by
Lorenz Books
Anness Publishing Inc.
27 West 20th Street
New York, NY 10011

www.lorenzbooks.com

This edition distributed in Canada
by Raincoast Books
9050 Shaughnessy Street
Vancouver
British Columbia V6P 6E5

A CIP catalogue record for this book is
available from the British Library.

Publisher: Joanna Lorenz
Project editor: Simona Hill
Step-by-step photography:
    Rodney Forte
Special photography: Nicky Dowey
Illustrator: Penny Brown
Designer: Margaret Sadler

Previously published as *Sewing* and as
part of a larger compendium, *The
Practical Encyclopedia of Sewing*

10 9 8 7 6 5 4 3 2 1

CONTENTS

INTRODUCTION

Whether you are interested in dressmaking or want to make your own soft furnishings, it is important to know and understand the basics of sewing. Starting with a list of equipment and detailed descriptions of the sewing machine and the many different kinds of fabric available, this book tells you everything you need to give you the confidence to create both successful garments and furnishing projects. Separate sections cover such introductory subjects as cutting out fabric  and basting, followed by hand and machine stitching. Basic techniques such as seams, bias binding and hemming, and more advanced techniques such as tucks and pleats, are all explained in clear step-by-step photographs. More inspirational photographs show the beautiful effects that are possible by using these techniques imaginatively.

Illustrations show the most popular hand embroidery and decorative smocking stitches. On a more practical level, buttonholes, buttons and fastenings of all kinds, including zippers, are given due attention. The book concludes with information on making basic cushions and curtains, accompanied by photographs of finished designs.

Making your own clothes and soft furnishings is extremely satisfying and also very economical. You can choose exactly the fabric you want and then, if you wish, finish your design with a decorative detail such as pin tucking or piping to make it truly unique. The most important thing, however, is to be able to judge which fabric is suitable for which pattern, what kind of seam to use, what weight of zipper, and what style of buttonhole. These are all questions that this book will be able to answer for you.

Sewing equipment

Are your needles the right size, your pins rust-free and your scissors sharp enough for fabric? Although most households have basic sewing equipment, it is worth checking that what you have is still in good condition before beginning to sew, and replacing things that are past their best.

1 Bodkin
A bodkin is used to thread elastic, cord or ribbon through casings.

2 Dressmaker's carbon and tracing wheel
These are used together to transfer construction markings to the wrong side of fabrics. Select a colour of carbon paper close to the fabric colour that is still visible, and always use white on white fabric (it shows as a dull line).

3 Fabric markers
Pencils are suitable for most hard-surfaced fabrics and can be brushed off with a stiff brush. Vanishing-ink pens wash out in water or fade over a few days. Tracing pens are used to draw a design on waxed paper that is transferred to fabric by ironing.

4 Fusible bonding web
This is a glue mesh that comes in various widths for sticking two layers of fabric together. The narrow bands (shown here) are useful for heavy-weight hems and facings, and the wider widths are used for appliqué.

5 Needles
Sharps (medium-length, all-purpose needles) are used for general hand sewing. For fine hand sewing, use the shorter, round-eyed "betweens". Hand-sewing needles are numbered according to thickness and range from 1–10, with 10 being the finest.

6 Pin cushion
A pin cushion is useful for holding the pins and needles you are using. A wrist pin cushion is convenient when you are fitting a garment.

7 Pins
Pins come in a surprising number of shapes and sizes. Use household pins for normal sewing, and wedding or lace pins for fine and delicate fabrics. Use ball-point pins for fine synthetic knit fabrics. Glass-headed pins are easy to see against fabrics.

8 Quilter's tape
Use this to mark accurate 5mm/¼in seam allowances.

9 Rouleau turner
Use this metal tool to turn through rouleau loops.

10 Safety pins
Use to hold thick layers of fabric together safely.

11 Scissors
You will need a large pair of drop-handle (bent-handle) scissors for cutting out, a medium pair for trimming seams or cutting small pieces of fabric and a small pair of sharp, pointed embroidery scissors for cutting threads and snipping into curves. Never cut paper with your dressmaking scissors – it dulls the blades. Pinking shears are used to finish raw edges on fabrics that do not unravel easily.

12 Seam ripper
This is a small cutting tool for undoing machine stitching mistakes or cutting buttonholes.

13 Tape measure
Tape measures should be marked with centimetres and inches on the same side for quick reference. Buy a 150cm/60in tape with metal tips in a material such as fibreglass that will not stretch. A small metal ruler with an adjustable guide is useful for pinning hems, tucks and buttonholes.

14 Tailor's chalk
Tailor's chalk is used to make temporary marks on the fabrics. Keep the edge sharp by shaving with medium scissors. Test before using on the right side of the fabric to ensure it will brush off.

15 Thimble
A thimble is worn on the middle finger of your sewing hand. Although awkward at first, persevere because it will prevent accidental needle pricks.

16 Thread
Use a shade of thread that matches your fabric, or go one shade darker. For best results choose a thread that matches the fibre content of your fabric. Tacking (basting) thread is cheap, and poorer-quality. Use button-hole twist or linen thread for tailored buttonholes, and strong thread for furnishing fabrics and hand quilting.

17 Tissue paper
When working with fine or delicate fabrics by machine, baste strips of tissue paper to each side of the seam before sewing. Tear off after use. Tissue paper is useful for lengthening or altering pattern pieces, and for transferring designs for embroidery.

The sewing machine

A sewing machine is one of the most expensive pieces of sewing equipment you will buy and you should take as much care choosing one as you would a washing machine or a car. Think about how much sewing you expect to do, not only next year but also ten or twenty years ahead.

Types of machine

All sewing machines sew a line of simple straight stitches, but new technology means there are many different types on the market.

Basic straight stitch and zigzag

The only basic straight stitch machines around today are antiques – but they still form beautiful stitches. Zigzag stitches move the needle from side to side. The stitch width and spacing can be altered.

Automatic

Automatic machines can move the fabric backwards and forwards while stitching to produce stretch stitches, saddle stitch and overlocking. They have special discs inside called pattern cams that produce a variety of elaborate embroidery stitches.

Electronic

Electronic machines (above) are smoother and more sophisticated than ordinary automatic machines. The motor is controlled electronically and stops as soon as you lift your foot from the pedal. The machine can also sew very slowly if required with the same power. Electronic machines can be automatic or computerized, having either cams or a computer to create the stitches.

Computerized

Computerized machines (above) are advanced models with silicon chips instead of pattern cams and are capable of a huge range of ornamental stitches. The stitches can be more complicated because the fabric can move in all directions. Touch-button panels or screens make them simple to use and some can stitch small motifs, or even your own designs when linked to a personal computer.

CHOOSING A SEWING MACHINE

Most people only ever use the straight stitch and zigzag on a sewing machine so think carefully before spending a lot of money on technology you don't really need. If you intend to make soft furnishings and curtains, a sturdy, secondhand flatbed machine may be best. Free-arm machines have a narrow arm that extends above the base to allow fabric to be moved around and are more suitable for dressmaking.

Take samples of different fabrics such as jersey, silk and denim with you and try them out folded double on the machines. Check that threading up is easy and the bobbin case is not difficult to handle. Check that the electric fittings and attachments are well made.

Find out what accessories are included and if parts are easily replaced. Finally check that the machine packs away easily and isn't too heavy. After all, they're supposed to be portable.

Spend some time reading the manual and becoming familiar with the different parts. If you haven't used a sewing machine before, practise sewing on paper without thread first. For this, set all the dials at zero except for the stitch length, which should be between 2 and 3. Using lined paper, go up and down the lines, then try stopping and reversing, and very slowly, following curves and circles. Once you are comfortable, practise the same techniques on a double layer of gingham fabric.

Know your machine

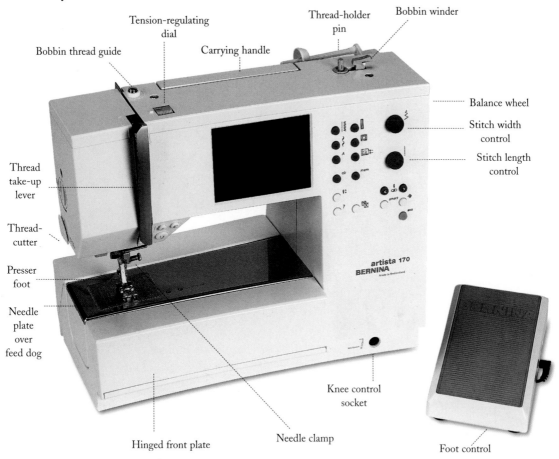

Tension-regulating dial

Thread-holder pin

Bobbin winder

Bobbin thread guide

Carrying handle

Balance wheel

Stitch width control

Stitch length control

Thread take-up lever

Thread-cutter

Presser foot

Needle plate over feed dog

artista 170
BERNINA
Made in Switzerland

Knee control socket

Hinged front plate

Needle clamp

Foot control

Balance wheel
This controls the sewing machine. On manual machines turn the wheel to lower the needle.

Bobbin winder
This allows you to fill the bobbin quickly and evenly.

Foot control/knee contol
This starts, stops and controls the speed that the machine stitches.

Needle clamp
This secures the shaft of the needle into the machine.

Needle plate
The needle plate surrounds the feed teeth and has a hole for the needle.

Presser foot
This holds the fabric flat on the needle plate so that a stitch can form.

Stitch length control
Use this to alter the length of straight stitch and the density of zigzag stitch.

Stitch width control
This controls the amount the needle moves sideways. Use a suitable presser foot so that the needle doesn't break.

Thread take-up lever
This feeds the correct amount of thread from the spool down through to the needle.

Tension-regulating dial
The tension dial alters the tension on the top thread.

Thread-cutter
This is situated at the back of the machine for cutting threads.

Thread-holder pin
This holds the reel of thread when filling the bobbin and stitching.

Threading the upper machine

Unless a machine is threaded in exactly the right sequence it won't work properly. Every machine has a slightly different sequence, but in all of them the thread goes between the tension discs and back up through the take-up lever before it is threaded through the needle.

Always have the take-up lever at its highest point before threading. This brings the needle up to its highest point and lines up all the mechanical parts inside the sewing machine ready for inserting the filled bobbin case. The manual accompanying your sewing machine should have a diagram showing the correct threading sequence for your particular model.

Horizontal thread-holders on the upper machine have a clip to hold the reel in position. The thread unwinds off one end of the stationary reel. Vertical thread-holders have a disc of felt to help the reel to spin around as the machine is working.

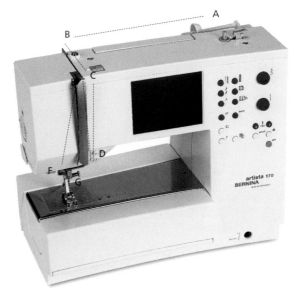

1 Fit the reel on to the thread-holder (A), making sure that the thread can come off freely. Take the thread round B, between the tension disks (C) and down under the first thread guide (D).

2 Put the thread into the top of the take-up lever (E) and then through the thread guides (F) leading down to the needle (G). Thread the needle from the grooved side (front to back).

Filling the bobbin

1 Fill the bobbin using the bobbin-winding mechanism on the machine. To begin, pass the end of the thread through one of the small holes in the side and fit it on to the spindle.

2 Click the bobbin-winding mechanism into place. This should automatically stop the machine from stitching – if not, you will have to loosen the stop motion knob on the hand wheel. The bobbin will fill automatically to the correct level.

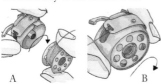

A   B

3 Insert the bobbin into the bobbin case (A) so that the thread is pulled back on itself through the spring (B).

4 Fit the bobbin case into the machine, holding the case by the lever on the back. The open lever locks the bobbin into the case.

5 Push the case into the socket until it clicks then release the lever. Close the cover. If it does not click, the mechanism inside is not aligned.

The bobbin thread

1 To raise the bobbin thread, thread the needle and hold the upper thread out to one side. Some machines have an automatic thread-lifting mechanism but otherwise turn the hand wheel forwards until the needle has gone down and up again. Pull the upper thread to bring the bobbin thread right out. Take both threads through the slot in the presser foot and out of the back.

Choosing a needle

Always select a machine needle to suit the thread and fabric you are using; this will reduce the likelihood of the needle breaking.

1 Universal needles

Universal sewing machine needles range in size from 70/9, used for fine fabrics, to 110/18, used for heavy-weight fabrics. Size 80/12 is ideal for medium-weight fabric. Keep a selection to hand and change your needle when using different weights of fabric. A fine needle will break if the fabric is too thick and a large needle will damage a fine fabric.

2 Ballpoint needles

Ballpoint needles are used for synthetic fabrics, jersey and elastic. They have a round end which pushes between the threads instead of piercing them. This type of needle can also be used with fine silks and delicate fabrics which may snag.

3 Twin needles

Twin needles consist of two needles fitted to the one shank. They are used to sew narrow, parallel lines or, when the machine tension is altered, to sew pin tucks. You can also buy special stretch twin needles for working on jersey fabrics. When threading the machine with these needles, you will need two reels of thread. For best results, take one thread down each side of the central tension disc.

4 Wing needles

Wing needles have a wide blade on each side of the shaft, which cuts a decorative groove in the fabric as you stitch.

5 Spring needles

A spring needle allows you to embroider without a darning foot or embroidery hoop because it stops the fabric from moving about.

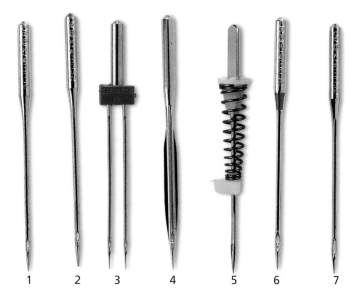

1   2   3   4   5   6   7

6 Embroidery needles

Embroidery needles have larger eyes than normal to allow sewing with a wide range of decorative threads. Some special embroidery needles have extremely large eyes for the thicker threads.

7 Top-stitch needles

Top-stitch needles have a very large eye to accommodate a thick, decorative thread.

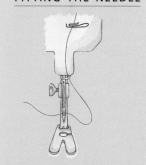

FITTING THE NEEDLE

Machine needles can only be fitted one way because they have a flat surface down one side (the shank) and a long groove down the other side (the shaft). When the needle is inserted, this groove should line up directly with the last thread guide. When the machine is in use, the thread runs down the groove and scores a unique channel into the metal. So when you change the type of thread, you should change your needle, too.

Machine feet

All machines have a number of interchangeable feet for different types of sewing. The most common ones are illustrated here but you can buy other specialist feet. These are designed for particular functions such as getting close to a zipper or guiding thread, cord or fabric while sewing.

Clear-view foot

Similar to the general-purpose foot, this foot allows you to see where you are stitching. It can be cut away or made from clear plastic. It can also be used for satin stitch because the underside of the foot is cut away to prevent the stitching from being flattened. Use it when working with bulky fabrics.

Hemming foot

A hemming foot has a curled piece of metal that turns a rolled hem on fine fabrics and feeds it under the needle. The hem can then be stitched with straight or fancy stitches.

Cording foot

This foot has a groove underneath which guides cord, round elastic or narrow ribbon under the needle for stitching.

Blind-hemming (blind-stitching) foot

This foot has a metal guide for a turned-back hem. It is possible to adjust the needle position so that just a few threads are caught when stitching.

General-purpose foot

The basic metal general-purpose foot shown is used for all general straight stitching and zigzag on ordinary fabrics.

Darning foot

A darning foot is used for machine darning and free-style machine embroidery. The feed teeth on the machine are always lowered and the fabric is held flat against the needle plate, using an embroidery hoop upside down. Set the stitch length at zero and sew straight stitch or zigzag with this foot.

Zipper foot

This allows you to stitch close to zipper teeth or piping. The needle can be adjusted to sew on either side. A special zipper foot is available to guide the teeth of invisible zippers.

Buttonhole foot

This foot has two grooves underneath to guide rows of satin stitch forwards and backwards, leaving a tiny gap between for cutting.

Spacing guide (seam guide)

This attachment can be used with a variety of different feet as long as the rod and clip fits. By sliding the rod along, a particular distance can be stitched accurately. This guide is useful for stitching curves and for machine quilting.

Stitch tension

A new machine will have the tension correctly set, with the dial at the marked centre point. Try out any stitches you intend to use on a sample of your fabric.

To check the tension, bring all the pattern and zigzag dials back to zero and set the stitch length between 2 and 3 for normal stitching. Place a folded strip of fabric on the needle plate, lower the needle into the fabric and sew a row of straight stitches. These should look exactly the same on both sides.

Above: The top and bottom threads lock together correctly in the middle of the fabric when the machine tension is correct.

Above: The top tension is loose and it is pulled to the wrong side of the fabric.

Above: The top thread tension is too tight.

Altering tension

To tighten the tension, turn the dial towards the lower numbers. To loosen it, turn towards the higher numbers. This will automatically affect the tension of the thread coming through the bobbin case. If the top tension dial is far from the centre, the spring on the bobbin case is probably wrong.

Only alter the lower tension as a last resort. You should be able to dangle the bobbin case without the thread slipping through. Shake the thread and the bobbin case should drop a little. Turn the screw on the side of the bobbin case slightly to alter the tension. Try out the stitching again on a sample of fabric and alter the top tension this time until the stitch is perfect.

Maintenance and trouble-shooting

Like a car, a sewing machine will only run well if it is used regularly and looked after. It needs to be oiled on a regular basis and cleaned out – this may be several times during the making of curtains or a garment. General maintenance only takes a few minutes but will ensure that your machine works well and lasts longer between services. Cleaning is essential when you change fabrics, especially if it is from a dark to a light-coloured one. Remove the sewing machine needle. Use a stiff brush to clean out the fluff (lint) along the route the top thread takes through the machine. Unscrew the needle plate and brush out any fluff from around the feed teeth. Remove the bobbin case to check that no thread is trapped in the mechanism.

Oil the machine from time to time using your handbook as a guide. Only use a couple of drops – too much oil can be damaging. Leave the machine overnight with a fabric pad beneath the presser foot and then wipe the needle before use. Some new machines are self-lubricating.

Even if you take care of your machine, problems can occur. Some of the more common problems are listed below.

The machine works too slowly

The machine may have two speeds and may be set on slow. More likely, it hasn't been used for a while and oil could be clogging the working parts. Run the machine without a needle for a minute to loosen all the joints. Check that the foot control is not obstructed. As a last resort, ask a dealer to check the tension belt.

No stitches form

Ensure the bobbin is full and inserted correctly. Check that the needle is facing in the right direction and threaded from the grooved side.

Above: Lace and velvet require extreme care when sewing. Always test a sample first to establish the correct tension.

The needle doesn't move

Check that the balance wheel is tight and that the bobbin winder is switched off. If the needle still doesn't move there may be thread trapped in the sewing hook behind the bobbin case. Remove the bobbin case and take hold of the thread end. Rock the balance wheel backwards and forwards until it comes out.

The machine jams

Rock the balance wheel gently to loosen the threads and take the fabric out. Remove the needle, unscrew the needle plate and brush out any fluff (lint). Alternatively check that the machine is correctly threaded and the fabric is far enough under the presser foot when beginning.

The needle bends or breaks

A needle will break if it hits the foot, bobbin case or needle plate on a machine. Check that you are using the correct foot. When using a zipper foot, a common mistake is forgetting to move the needle to the left or right for straight stitching or zigzag. Check the bobbin case is inserted properly. Make sure the take-up lever is at its highest point before fitting.

A needle that has been bent will break if it hits the needle plate. To avoid bent needles, sew slowly over

pins and thick seams. A needle will also bend if there is a knot in the thread or if the fabric is pulled through the machine faster than the machine is sewing.

Fabric does not feed through

This can happen when the feed teeth are lowered in the darning position. Close zigzag or embroidery stitches will bunch up in the general-purpose foot, so change the foot to one that is cut away underneath to allow the stitches to feed through.

The stitches are different lengths

Check whether the needle is blunt or unsuitable for the fabric and that it is inserted correctly. Try stitching with the needle in the left and right position. On fine fabrics, put tissue paper under the presser foot.

The top thread keeps breaking

Manufacturers recommend that you change needles every time you change the type of thread. This is because each thread type scores a unique channel through the needle groove which will cause a different type of thread to snag and break. Label your needle packet to indicate what type of thread to use with each needle. This is particularly important when doing machine embroidery. Check that you are using the correct thread and type of needle for the fabric. A knot or slub in the thread may also cause the thread to break.

The bobbin thread breaks

Check that the bobbin case is inserted correctly, has not been overfilled and the thread has no knots in it. Also check the bobbin case mechanism for trapped fluff. Occasionally, the spring on the bobbin case is too tight for the thread and the tension screw has to be loosened – refer to your user manual for instructions.

Understanding fabrics

The most exciting part of sewing, whether you are dressmaking or sewing soft furnishings, is choosing the fabric. Making the right choice is essential for the success of the finished project. The type of fabric will affect the drape and handling of the item as well as its life-span.

At one time it was easy to choose fabrics as wool blanketing, cotton lawn, viscose rayon prints and silk dupion were instantly recognizable. Even polyester and nylon fabrics were distinct. But recent advances in technology have made it almost impossible to tell what a fabric is made from just by looking at it.

Fibres form the basis of any fabric. They are either fused together to make a fabric like felt and fleece, or twisted together to form a yarn that is then knitted or woven. There are a huge number of different fabrics on sale today and the majority are a mix of several fibres. To make things easier for the consumer, it is now law for each fabric to carry a label listing the type and proportions of all the

different fibres it contains where these make up more than 5 per cent. If a smaller quantity affects the behaviour of the main fibre, it must be listed too: for example, 1 per cent Lycra or Spandex will add a fair degree of stretch to a fabric and will be included on the label.

Natural fibres
These develop naturally in a fibrous form from either a plant or animal source. Cotton, linen, wool and silk are the most well known but the group also includes hemp, used for sacking or hessian (burlap), and luxury animal hair fibres such as mohair, alpaca, cashmere, angora, vicuna and camel. Each natural fibre has an unmistakable inherent character that

is reflected in the fabric. For example, wool is soft and warm, cotton is cool and crisp, silk has a dry, papery texture and linen a wonderful sheen.

Man-made and synthetic fibres
Until the mid-nineteenth century, natural fibres were the only materials available for fabric production. As silk was expensive, scientists experimented with the aim of producing a cost-effective "artificial silk". The first rayon – made in 1892 – heralded a new era for the textile industry.

Man-made and synthetic fabrics are not the same – each has distinct properties. Man-made fibres are produced from natural products, primarily cellulose, although some rare fabrics use regenerated milk protein. Synthetic fabrics are made entirely from chemical sources.

Recent developments have refined the quality of man-made and synthetic fibres, making them indispensable to today's fashion and sportswear designers. Cosy fleece jackets are made from a crimped 100 per cent polyester fibre. Lycra and Spandex, two highly elastic synthetic fibres, have transformed the leisure-wear market. The range of luxury fabrics has increased, too, as man-made fibres such as Cupro have been improved to produce exquisite fabrics with a soft, silky texture. Not only are these fabrics more accessible, many are machine washable.

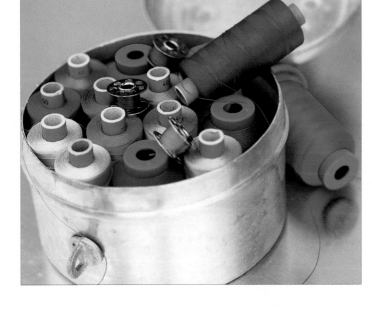

Left: Brightly coloured rayon machine embroidery threads show how well this man-made fibre takes dyes.

Cotton fabrics

Cotton fibres are harvested from the seed pods of the *Gossypium* plant. The fibres vary in quality and length depending on where the plant is grown, resulting in a vast range of cotton fabrics from the finest Swiss organdie to the coarsest Indian cottons. Cotton fabrics are highly absorbent, with wet strength, making them suitable for frequent laundering at high temperatures.

Batiste
A soft, finely woven fabric originally made from linen. It is usually only made in white or pastel colours and is used for handkerchiefs, lingerie and christening robes.

Calico
This is a generic term for plain-woven fabrics that are heavier than muslin. It is generally a neutral colour but can be bleached white. Calico is a cheap fabric, used for backing, linings and some home furnishings.

Canvas
This rather stiff, warp-faced cloth is made in different weights for interlinings, tents or deckchairs. Needlepoint canvas is an open-weave fabric used for embroidery.

Chambray
This is a medium-weight, plain-weave fabric woven from coloured warps and white wefts. It has the appearance of soft, stone-washed denim and can be striped or checked.

Cheesecloth (Butter muslin)
This is a sheer, plain-weave, white fabric that is used as a light-weight interfacing, as a pressing cloth or as a net curtain. It was originally used to line tins and baskets for draining the whey from soft cheese. Care must be taken when cutting out as the fabric is very loosely woven.

Chintz
This is a plain-woven fabric with one glazed surface. It is often printed with floral or natural motifs and used for soft furnishings.

Corduroy
This is a pile fabric that has cut weft threads which form cords running the length of the fabric. The cords can be fine or heavy, creating different weight fabrics, such as needlecord and jumbo cord. Corduroy can be made on plain or twill weave and can be printed.

Damask
This is a reversible, jacquard-weave fabric. The fabric is woven on complex jacquard looms that create the intricate, embossed surface. It is flatter than brocade, which is woven in the same way.

Denim
Originating in Nimes in France, this strong twill weave is woven with indigo-dyed warps and white weft threads. It was traditionally used for jeans, but is now also used for furnishings. The distinctive washed-out look of denim occurs because the dye fades with each wash.

Drill
This strong twill weave has a similar weight and feel to denim. It is known as khaki when dyed that shade.

Flannelette (Cotton flannel)
This is an imitation of wool flannel. Softly woven weft threads are brushed to produce a fluffy surface with a warm feel. When flame-proofed, it is used for children's nightwear.

Right: 1 voile; 2 knitted cotton; 3 chambray; 4 ticking; 5 denim; 6 muslin; 7 cotton print; 8 flannelette (cotton flannel); 9 stone-washed denim; 10 moleskin; 11 winceyette; 12 gingham; 13 zephyr (shirtings).

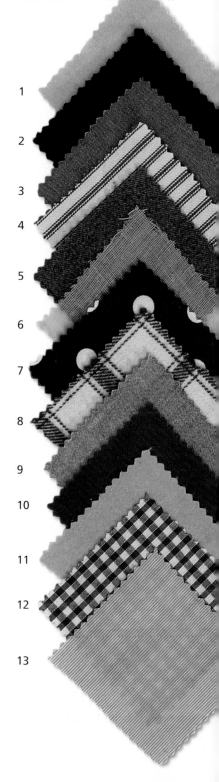

1
2
3
4
5
6
7
8
9
10
11
12
13

Left: Printed cotton fabrics are ideal for dresses, shirts and skirts.

Gingham
A firm, light-weight, plain-weave fabric that is woven with dyed yarns to produce the distinctive light, medium and dark checks. This is a hard-wearing fabric, commonly used for smocked garments and home furnishings.

Hessian (Burlap)
This is a coarse, heavy, plain-weave fabric made from jute, cotton or linen. It is used for sacking or as a backing for upholstery and rugs, since it is hard-wearing. It is mostly used where it is not seen. Jute is a cellulose fibre from India.

Indian cotton
The heavy weft threads are a distinctive feature of Indian cotton fabrics. The soft, bulky fabric is often dyed, printed or woven in stripes and checks. It is used for soft furnishings.

Jersey
This is a knitted fabric that originated on the island of Jersey. It is constructed in a tube shape in stockinette stitch. Natural-coloured cotton jersey is used for making rag dolls and a loose woven version is sold as a dish cloth (kitchen cloth).

Knitted cotton
Machine-knitted cotton is commonly used for summer sweaters and leisure wear. The fabric doesn't have the same "give" as knitted wool but is often blended with Lycra for sportswear.

Lace
Cotton lace is a heavy open-work fabric used for table linen, bridal wear and home furnishings. The threads are twisted, looped or knotted into complicated patterns on a complex loom that reads punched card patterns just like a musical organ.

Moleskin
This is a fairly hard-wearing, warm fabric used originally for workmen's trousers but now a fashion fabric available in a range of rich colours. It has the appearance of smooth suede or close-cut velvet.

Muslin
This is a term used for a wide range of soft, plain-weave fabrics that can be decorated with spots or embroidery. In the United Kingdom muslin is generally thought of as a sheer, roughly woven fabric, whereas in the United States it is a closer woven fabric used for patchwork.

Organdie
This very fine, transparent fabric is treated with sulphuric acid to produce the characteristic crisp finish. It is used as a luxury dress fabric, as a stiffening interfacing, or for exquisite, fine household linen goods.

Piqué
Piqué refers to the raised cord weave that runs lengthways down a fabric. It can be embroidered to produce the characteristic holes and surface embroidery of broderie anglaise.

Printed cottons
Printed fabrics are not reversible as the dye colour does not penetrate completely through to the other side. Cotton is absorbent and takes colour well. There is a vast range of printed patterned cottons in several weights suitable for dress fabrics, patchwork and home furnishings.

Scrim
This is a light-weight, open-weave fabric used as an interfacing, for pulled thread embroidery or for curtains. It can be made in cotton or linen and is often used for theatre backdrops.

Stone-washed denim

This is normal denim that has a faded, well-worn look. It has a soft feel achieved either by tumbling the denim with pumice stones or treating it with chemicals.

Ticking

This is a strong, durable twill-weave fabric with a distinctive lengthways coloured stripe. It was until recently purely a utilitarian fabric, but now it is a fashionable fabric used for kitchenware and soft furnishings.

Towelling (Terrycloth)

This distinctive, absorbent, loop-pile fabric is generally made from cotton. It can be woven or knitted, with the pile on one or both sides.

Below: Gingham is a traditional woven cotton fabric that has recently become fashionable again. It is available in various widths as ribbon or as a fabric.

Voile

This is a sheer, light-weight fabric with a crisp feel. It has a plain, open weave with tightly twisted fibres. Voile is usually starched to retain its crisp feel.

Winceyette

This medium-weight fabric is woven with a plain or twill weave, and is brushed on each side for warmth. It has a similar appearance to flannelette (cotton flannel). It is flame-proofed when used for children's nightwear.

Zephyr (Shirtings)

This is a light-weight, finely woven fabric made primarily for shirting. It is either plain or twill weave and often has woven stripes or checks.

Right: 1 damask; 2 muslin; 3 lace; 4 batiste; 5 jersey; 6 organdie; 7 Indian cotton; 8 calico; 9 velvet; 10 piqué/broderie anglaise; 11 scrim; 12 hessian (burlap).

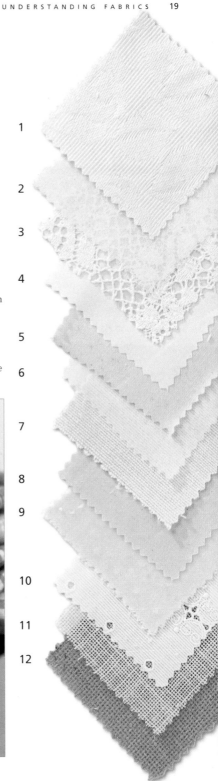

1
2
3
4
5
6
7
8
9
10
11
12

Woollen fabrics

Wool fibres come from the fleece of a sheep. The quality is determined by the breed of sheep and the length of the fibres used. Wool fibres have a natural crimp that helps the fabric to shed creases, but also allows folds to be pressed in with heat and steam. There is a wide variety of wool fabrics divided into two distinct groups – woollens and worsteds.

Woollens are made from fibres that are simply carded then spun. The resulting yarn is bulky and made into fabrics such as blazer cloth, flannel and tweed. Worsteds are much finer, made from combed fibres spun into a tight, smooth yarn. Fabrics such as tweed, gabardine and the new "cool wool" are made from worsted.

Blanket/Flannel

Blanketing is woven in plain weave then brushed to raise the fibres on both surfaces to produce a soft pile fabric. It is light-weight but warm, and ideal for bedding or coats.

Challis

This is a light-weight, soft, worsted wool fabric woven with a plain weave. It is suitable for shirts and blouses.

Cool wool

This fabric is woven from worsted wool and is smooth and light-weight. It has an unusual diagonal basket weave on the right side and a plain weave on the wrong side.

Crêpe

Wool crêpe has a soft feel with a delicate, pebbly surface. This is achieved by weaving in a random manner to produce top threads floating in an irregular pattern.

Above: Wool is a versatile fabric that can be made into a wide variety of fabrics and yarns. The design and colour are normally introduced by weaving two or more differently coloured threads together.

Dog's tooth check

The unusual weave pattern in this fabric is a variation of a twill weave. Hound's tooth check is a larger version of the dog's tooth check.

Double-face knit

This reversible fabric is made by knitting two layers and holding them together with binding threads. The fabric is less likely to curl than normal knit fabrics.

Twill weave

Herringbone and shepherd's check are variations of the twill weave with distinctive patterns.

Wool blends

Man-made fibres with a similar texture to wool are blended with it to produce a wide range of less expensive suiting or coat-weight fabric.

Left: 1 knitted; 2 wool and mohair; 3 wool and silk; 4 coat weight; 5 crêpe; 6 coat weight; 7 dog's tooth check; 8 cool wool; 9 challis; 10 twill weave; 11 herringbone weave; 12 hound's tooth check; 13 wool blend; 14 blanket; 15 flannel; 16 fancy weave.

Silk fabrics

Cultivated silk is produced by the silk worm (caterpillar) of the *Bombyx mori* moth. The silk filament is very smooth and strong, creating fine fabrics with excellent draping qualities. Its strength allows sheer fabrics such as chiffon and georgette to be produced. Wild Tussah silk is produced by the caterpillar of the *Antheraea* moth. The filament of wild silk is very irregular, producing the well-known slub appearance.

Crêpe-backed satin

This beautiful fabric combines two weaves to produce a lovely soft fabric that drapes well. The satin and crêpe weaves are combined to give a crêpe fabric on one side, with floating satin threads on the right side.

Dupion

This has an irregular texture that is woven from silk produced by double cocoons, created when two silk worms nest together. This gives the fabric its characteristic large slubs. It is a popular bridal fabric.

Futi

Silk futi is a beautiful soft shirt-weight fabric woven in a twill weave. The silk has been treated to produce a slightly brushed surface that gives it a warm feel.

Georgette

This is a sheer, dull crinkly fabric that is heavier than chiffon. It has a plain weave that is textured by crêpe, twisted yarns. It has a soft handle and is used for evening wear.

Habotai

Habotai is a general term for fine, soft, plain-weave silk fabrics that have been de-gummed. The lightest weights are used for lining fabric, but heavier weights are sold as dress fabric.

Organza

A sheer, stiff, plain-weave cloth made from continuous filament silk in the gum. The threads are highly twisted to produce a crisp finish. Silk and metallic threads can be woven together to produce metallic organza.

Ottoman

This plain-weave fabric has a heavy corded effect caused by thicker weft threads. Normally used for evening wear, heavier-weight Ottoman cloths are suitable for tailoring.

Satin

The satin weave leaves long floating threads on the right side of this smooth fabric. It is available in various weights and qualities, with the heaviest known as duchesse satin.

Shantung

Shantung is a rough plain-weave cloth originally hand woven in China from wild Tussah silk.

Right: 1 satin; 2 duchesse satin; 3 dupion; 4 satin; 5 organza; 6 Ottoman; 7 crêpe-backed satin; 8 georgette; 9 habotai; 10 futi; 11 shantung; 12 duchesse satin.

Left: This soft luxury fabric takes dye easily and is available in a vibrant palette of intense colours.

1
2
3
4
5
6
7
8
9
10
11
12

1
2
3
4
5
6
7
8
9
10
11
12
13

Linen fabrics

Linen fibres are found in the stem of the flax plant *Linum usitatissimum*. Jute and hemp are also obtained from the stem of plants. Flax fibres are extremely long – about 1m/1yd – when they are extracted from the plant but lose some length during processing. The long fibres give linen its characteristic sheen. Linen is more absorbent than cotton and makes good tea towels (dish cloths) or table linen, but has a lower resistance to abrasion. Originally, linen was bleached after weaving but a process has been developed for bleaching the fibres, which allows them to be blended with other fibres. Linens range from fine batiste for handkerchiefs to heavy-weight Jacquard suiting.

Batiste

This fine, antique, white Irish linen woven in a plain weave is "calendered", a process that smooths the surface and imparts a crisp, lustrous finish. It is used for making handkerchiefs, lingerie and fine household linens.

Left: 1 Jacquard weave; 2 batiste; 3 raw even-weave; 4 white even-weave; 5 bleached raw; 6 hand-woven; 7 twill weave; 8 scrim; 9 linen and silk; 10 stripe; 11 raw; 12 antique white; 13 cork.

Even-weave linen

This raw linen fabric has been woven in a "square" weave with exactly 31 threads running in each direction. The care required for weaving to such exacting standards makes it more expensive than ordinary linen. It is available as a raw or bleached fabric in a wide range of colours. The fabric is used for counted-thread embroidery.

Hand-woven

This rough-textured fabric is woven from a variety of thicknesses of yarn, producing a soft, hand-woven look. It is treated to make it more crease-resistant than normal linen.

Jacquard

This 60 per cent linen/40 per cent cotton blend is woven on a Jacquard loom to produce the complex weave.

Pointed twill

The bleached linen yarn is woven in a broken twill pattern to produce this attractive pattern of zigzags and stripes. The lustre of the linen fibres makes the weave particularly effective.

Below: Linen has a wonderful slubby texture which is often copied in other fibres.

Hair

This includes any animal fibre other than sheep's wool or silk. Two types of fibre are collected: the long outer coat and the soft downy undercoat.

Alpaca

The alpaca is closely related to the llama. It produces fairly fine and soft fibres which can grow to 60cm/24in long if the animal is not sheared. The longer fibres are sometimes used for pile fabrics. Because the fibres are difficult to bleach they are used in their natural colour range of white, fawn, brown and black.

Angora

Angora comes from the long-haired angora rabbit. The fibres can be up to 7.5cm/3in long and are brushed from the animal. They are very soft and have a silky texture.

Camel

Camel hair is the long, downy undercoat produced by the Bactrian camel. It is a soft but strong fibre that grows to about 16cm/6¼in in length.

Below: Because hair fibres are the most expensive fibres, they are often blended with other types to produce more affordable luxury yarns and fabrics.

Like sheep's wool, the fibre has surface scales that allow the fabric to be felted. It is used for overcoats and dressing gowns in its original colour because it is difficult to bleach.

Cashmere

Fibres from the downy undercoat of the Tibetan goat are very fine and grow to about 9cm/3½in long. Cashmere is soft and warm and is used to make luxury knitwear and shawls.

Mohair

These soft, smooth fibres come from the angora goat. The lustrous fibres have relatively few surface scales and are generally blended with worsted wool. Mohair fibres can be up to 30cm/12in long and are made into long-pile knitted or woven fabrics.

Vicuna

The soft hair of the wild vicuna, a small type of llama, is the finest of all the animal fibres. The fibres are about 5cm/2in long and are generally used in their natural colour.

Right: 1 cashmere; 2 vicuna; 3 alpaca; 4 camel; 5 alpaca; 6 cashmere; 7 vicuna; 8 vicuna; 9 cashmere; 10 wool and cashmere.

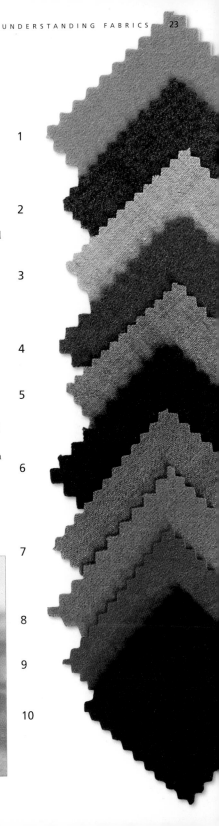

1

2

3

4

5

6

7

8

9

10

Synthetic fabrics

Synthetic fibres are produced entirely from chemical sources. Different fibre types are produced from different chemicals: nylon is a derivative of coke and tar, while polyester is a by-product of the petroleum industry. The range of fabrics is increasing as new ways to texture and process the raw filaments are developed. Synthetic fibres can melt and must be ironed on a cool heat setting.

Felt
Made with acrylic fibres or with wool, the soft, bulky fibre is made into felt by the application of heat, moisture and pressure.

Fleece
As the fabric is knitted, coarse yarn is laid in, then raised or fluffed up between teasels. Elastomeric yarn such as Lycra is often added to improve the stretch.

Jersey
Fine jersey fabric can be knitted from crimped nylon to produce a crêpe effect. The addition of an elastomeric yarn gives it a high degree of stretch.

Lycra
Lycra is a trade name for an elastomeric fibre made from polyurethane. This sheer fabric can stretch to double its length.

Microfibre
This beautiful, very fine polyester fibre looks like a luxury natural fabric, is easy to care for and has good crease resistance.

Left: 1 acrylic felt; 2 polyester; 3 Lycra;
4 polyester fleece; 5 suedette and Spandex;
6 taffeta; 7 Microfibre; 8 nylon net;
9 nylon velvet; 10 nylon jersey;
11 basket-weave polyester; 12 printed polyester; 13 polyester peachskin.

Mock peau-de-soie
This finely ribbed fabric is made from Microfibre to emulate the exquisite peau-de-soie silk fabrics. It has superb draping and handling qualities with good crease resistance.

Mock suede
This smooth, soft fabric has a tight twill weave that has been raised on the right side by rubbing with carborundum. This process produces a napped surface. Spandex, an elastomeric fibre, adds a degree of stretch.

Nylon net
Nylon is a hard fibre with poor draping qualities. These apparently negative aspects are used to produce a stiff net that is ideal for making petticoats and costumes.

Polyester
Polyester is a generic term for a range of fabrics with good crease resistance and easy-care properties.

Taffeta
This crisp fabric has fine weft-way ribs, due to the weft and warp threads being of similar weight. The slub effect is used to emulate silk.

Below: Brightly coloured felt can be made from acrylic or wool fibres.

Man-made fabrics

The majority of man-made fibres are made from regenerated cellulose, which is the main component of cotton, linen, jute and hemp. The fibre is produced by extruding a solution of cellulose through a spinneret. The cellulose is then coagulated in filament form in an acid bath. The variety of man-made fibres is produced by modifying this basic procedure. Man-made fabrics are being improved and introduced all the time. They include rayon, viscose rayon, Cupro, cellulose acetate and Modal. Man-made fibres are often blended so that their combined properties make a fabric with improved handling and feel.

Acetate

This fabric is used as a lining. Made from cellulose acetate, it has a silky feel and excellent draping qualities.

Cupro

The soft, draping qualities of Cupro have been given an added dimension by weaving to create the characteristic cord effect of a piqué fabric.

Jersey

This fine jersey fabric has been blended with elastane to create a very stretchy fabric. It is much finer than cotton jersey and has a lovely soft feel.

Modal

This ribbed fabric has a watermarked effect known as moiré, produced by applying heat and steam while pressing the fabric between engraved rollers. The flattened areas reflect light in a different way, producing the effect.

Printed viscose

Viscose rayon has a good affinity for dyes and so a wide variety of boldly coloured, printed viscose dress fabrics is available. The viscose rayon creases readily unless specially treated.

Tencel gaberdine

Gaberdine is a firm, tightly woven twill fabric often made from fine worsted wool. Tencel is a strong man-made fibre with a similar feel to wool without the same shrinkage problems.

Velvet

This beautiful velvet fabric has a viscose rayon pile on a Cupro base fabric. Cupro has a soft lustre and good draping qualities. The viscose rayon makes a wonderful soft pile with a high sheen.

Viscose acetate

Viscose rayon and acetate blended together produce a fabric that is less likely to crease and takes a stronger colour of dye. The silk-like appearance of acetate is softened and the draping quality improved.

Right: 1 viscose acetate; 2 Tencel gaberdine; 3 polyester and viscose; 4 Tencel gaberdine; 5 cellulose acetate; 6 viscose and Cupro velvet; 7 viscose rayon jersey and elastane; 8 eyelet embroidery viscose rayon; 9 Cupro piqué; 10 Modal moiré; 11 printed viscose rayon.

Left: Manufacturing processes produce a vast range of man-made fabrics, many of which handle similarly to natural fibres.

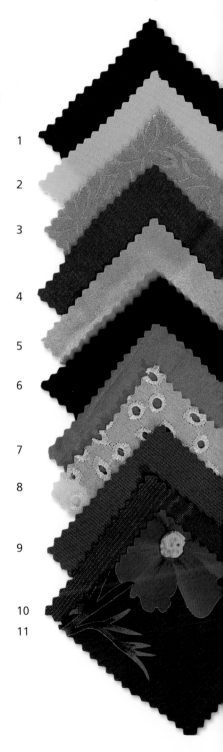

1
2
3
4
5
6
7
8
9
10
11

Decorative fabrics

In recent years fabric production has advanced with the constant introduction of new fibres and the innovative way these fibres are being used. There is a huge range of decorative fabrics for evening wear, bridal wear and fun outfits. The majority of these fabrics require special handling in the way they are cut out, how they are stitched or the way they are cleaned.

Cotton lace

This is much heavier in weight than other lace fabrics. It is used for bridal wear and table linen. The edges are usually cut following the motifs of the lace rather than being hemmed. Lace can be fine and delicate or thick and heavy in appearance.

Cotton organdie

Organdie is a sheer, plain-weave fabric. The cotton yarn is tightly spun before weaving to give the fabric a very crisp feel.

Left: 1 imitation fur; 2 crushed organza; 3 PVC; 4 metallic organza; 5 paper lamé; 6 suede; 7 printed velvet; 8 nylon and lurex net; 9 vinyl crocodile skin.

Crushed organza

This fabric is made in the same way as metallic organza but has the creases set in to produce an unusual crimped fabric. It is used for scarves and evening wear.

Devoré velvet

This is a luxury fabric with a pile surface that has been "burnt out" in sections to create a velvet pattern on a sheer background.

Fun fur

The polypropylene base for this fabric softens at low temperatures and can be shaped easily to make hats. Fun fur is also used to make soft toys, soft furnishings and fashion garments.

Imitation fur

Advances in the production of imitation fur have shown how realistic it can be made to look. Imitation fur is light and is easy to stitch. The fur fabric shown has a knitted backing.

Below: Lace is made in different weights and fibres. The heavy, dress-weight lace shown here is used mainly for evening or bridal wear.

1
2
3
4
5
6
7
8
9

Above: Three different textures – velvet, net and satin – are combined here to produce an exquisitely simple bridesmaid's dress.

Lurex net

Nylon and Lurex yarns are knitted together to form a loose, open net. It is used for evening wear, hat veiling and for craft projects.

Metallic organza

The organza shown here has red silk threads in one direction and gold metallic threads in the other.

Metallic printed jersey

The silver appearance on this fabric is produced by printing small metallic dots over the jersey fabric. Despite being a stretch fabric, the metallic surface is distorted if pulled too much.

Nylon organza

The nylon shown here has been woven with Lurex threads to create an unusual checked organza. The nylon gives the fabric a rather harsh feel.

Panné velvet

Panné is a pressure finish for velvet that flattens the pile, giving it a lustrous sheen. As this fabric is knitted, it has to be cut and stitched as a nap and stretch fabric.

Paper lamé

Lamé is a fabric made of metallic threads and another fibre. In this case the other fibre is nylon, which gives the fabric a hard, crisp feel like paper.

Polythene (Plastic)

This plastic material is used primarily for shower curtains. It can be stitched, but care must be taken so that it doesn't rip along the stitch line.

Polyvinyl chloride (PVC)

This plastic is used as a coating on fabric to make it waterproof. It is used for rainwear, tablecloths and bags.

Sequin fabric

This polyester and nylon jersey fabric is knitted with a Lurex thread and then has small plastic sequins fused on to the surface. Stitch straight seams, between the sequins if possible.

Suede and leather

This is a natural fabric prepared from animal skin. Suede has a rough texture, whereas leather has a smooth surface. It is used for simply styled clothing, shoes, bags and furnishings. It is sold as part or whole skins.

Velour

This fabric can be knitted or woven and has a dense, short pile. The velour shown has a knitted, nylon backing and a multi-colour pile.

Vinyl

This is a thermoplastic material that can be moulded and heat-set into shape, such as a crocodile skin surface. The plastic is quite stiff and is used for handbags or luggage.

Right: 1 panné velour; 2 cotton lace; 3 organdie; 4 nylon and Lurex organza; 5 imitation fur; 6 dévoré velvet; 7 sequin fabrics; 8 polythene (plastic); 9 metallic printed jersey; 10 PVC.

Above: 1 laminated; 2 knitting; 3 net; 4 stitch binding; 5 weaving; 6 felting.

Below: This felt hat demonstrates how this sturdy fabric can be manipulated.

Fabric structures

Fabrics made from natural fibres have been in existence from the earliest times and over the years a wide variety of different cloths have been produced, each with specific characteristics. Some construction methods, such as crochet and hand knitting, are labour-intensive and only suitable for small-scale operations or for making luxury fabrics. Other methods have been highly mechanized to produce vast quantities of fabric.

Weaving, knitting, lace-making, braiding and felting are the more traditional, instantly recognizable methods of textile construction but stitch-bonding, laminating and needling are also used to create a wide range of fabrics.

Bonded fibre fabrics

These fabrics are generally used for interfacings, wadding (batting), disposable garments or cleaning cloths. They are not, however, suitable for general use because of their poor recovery and draping qualities.

The fibres are made into a thick random layer called a "batt" and held together by several different methods. They can be fused with an adhesive, stitched together with rows of parallel stitching or needled. This last process uses rows of barbed needles to entangle the fibres together, creating a light-weight felted fabric used for quilting.

Braiding

Braids are traditionally created by weaving a large number of warp threads together. The threads are woven in a bias direction to produce a narrow, interlaced band. Ric-rac braid (shown at the top of the samples above) is made in this way. Heavier furnishing braids are woven using warp and weft threads, with the two groups of threads lying at right angles to each other.

Crochet

Hand crochet is produced using a single hook and a length of thread. Solid and lacy fabrics can be created by making the loops in different combinations. Filet crochet is a pictorial crochet technique that uses treble and chain stitches to create a design. The background has a square chain stitch mesh and the design is made from blocks of treble stitches. The yarn used for crocheting is generally smooth and tightly spun so that the hook catches it cleanly. Hand crochet was traditionally used to make mats, rugs and crochet lace borders, but machines can now speed up the process and crocheted garments are much easier to handle.

Felting

Felt is traditionally made by matting fibres together by applying heat, moisture, friction and pressure. Felting doesn't require any special equipment. Felted fabrics do not fray but they have no elasticity and will not return to their original shape once stretched. Modern craft felts are made from crimped synthetic fibres such as acrylic and polyester, and are created using bonded fibre techniques.

Knitting

Some knitted garments are still made by hand but are labour-intensive and expensive to produce. Machine-knitted fabrics have become more widespread as technology has increased the variety of yarns that can be stitched by machine. Weft knitting is similar to hand knitting but is worked from one side only, either in a circular machine to produce a tube of fabric or on a flat-bed machine. Warp knitting is slightly different. A set of warp threads are worked parallel to each other and interconnected to produce knitted fabric. Knitted fabrics are very elastic and this can be increased by the introduction of an elastomeric yarn.

Laminating

This is a process where two layers are stuck together to improve stability or warmth, or to provide weatherproofing. Laminating gives fabrics a different end use. A lining can be fused to a fabric before cutting to reduce construction costs, and a thin layer of plastic can be fused to a fabric base to provide a waterproof barrier. Imitation leather, PVC and other vinyls are all made in this way.

Netting

Netting is a versatile construction method that produces fabrics as diverse as fishing nets and delicate lace. There are two hand methods of lace-making – bobbin lace and needle-lace. Machine-made lace uses the same basic method as bobbin lace, where threads are twisted together to form a mesh of holes. The hexagonal mesh of stiff net is produced on a Leavers lace machine. Plain net and tulle is made on a bobbinet machine. Narrow and fabric-width lace are made by a similar method on Leavers lace machines.

Weaving

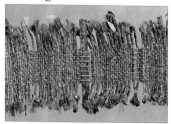

Woven fabrics are produced by interlacing two sets of threads together at right angles to each other. The warp threads are stronger and run lengthways down the fabric. The weft threads run across the fabric. The way these threads interlace produces the weave, which influences the appearance of the fabric and the way it handles.

Several fabrics are known by their weave, such as gaberdine, satin, twill and poplin. Other woven fabrics look and handle quite differently even though they use the same weave. Decorative weaves such as Leno, Dobby and Jacquard are produced on more complex looms. Leno weaving produces a lacy, open weave, whereas finely textured fabrics such as piqué are created on a Dobby loom, and brocades and damasks on a Jacquard loom.

Above: This evening jacket is trimmed with braid to give a crisp, decorative finish.

Linings, interfacings and threads

In sewing, success depends primarily on the quality and cut of the fabric to drape or lie in a certain way, but sometimes it is necessary to support the fabric with an interfacing or lining. The sewing thread should always be chosen to suit the type of fabric.

Linings

Although linings are normally hidden from view, it is important to choose these undercover fabrics carefully. You need to pick one that will complement the outer fabric in weight and colour. Lining fabrics are now made to suit every eventuality. They can be woven or knitted and stretch or non-stretch.

With linings the fibre content is important, too. Pick a lining with a complementary fibre to the outer fabric. Man-made linings such as

Bremsilk or an acetate taffeta will work better with a natural fibre than a polyester taffeta. If the outer fabric can be washed, make sure the lining is washable too. Finally, select a lining that will move in the same way as the main fabric and one that will be as durable as the outer fabric. Seams in an ordinary lining will split during wear if the outer fabric is stretchy. A less durable lining fabric will wear out before the outer fabric.

Dressmaking patterns usually have separate pattern pieces for the lining.

Below: 1 stretch lining; 2 Bremsilk; 3 acetate taffeta; 4 Eton taffeta.

Right: A contrast lining has been used to effect inside the wide sleeves of this gown.

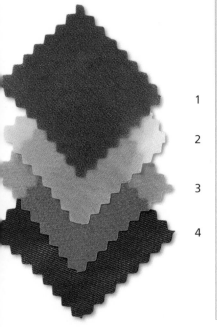

1

2

3

4

LINING FABRICS

Acetate taffeta
A basic general-purpose lining that can be hand washed or dry cleaned. It has a medium weight and crisp handle.

Nylon jersey lining
A stretchy, light-weight translucent fabric, suitable for see-through fabrics. It has an anti-static finish and can be hand washed.

Stretch lining
An acetate fabric with 4 per cent Lycra added to give it stretch. It is an ideal lining for suiting fabrics, especially those with a percentage of Lycra added. Dry cleaning is recommended.

Bremsilk
A light-weight artificial silk lining made from Cupro. It is a wonderfully soft, lining fabric that handles well with natural fibres. It can be hand washed or dry cleaned.

Eton taffeta
A lighter-weight, anti-static lining that can be washed to 50°C/122°F or dry cleaned. It is made from 100 per cent polyester.

Shot twill
This is an attractive suit lining fabric made from a mixture of viscose and acetate fibres. It is a heavier-weight lining with a soft feel. It must be dry cleaned.

Interfacings

Areas such as collars, cuffs and lapels are interfaced to hold their shape. Larger areas are interfaced to give support and add body to the outer fabric. Commercial patterns have separate pieces for interfacing, which is normally cut without seams and sewn or ironed in.

Interfacing is available in black or white, and in light, medium or heavy weights – which one you choose will depend on the outer fabric colour and the amount of support required.

Iron or sew?

Interfacing is either woven or non-woven. Non-woven interfacing has no grain and can be cut in any direction. Where possible, iron-on interfacing should be attached to the facing rather than the outer fabric.

Standard interfacings are really only suitable for plain, cotton synthetic blends. Soft stretch and reinforced non-woven interfacings are also available for use with other fabrics.

1
2
3
4
5
6

Above: 1 fusible stitch-reinforced; 2 medium-weight; 3 light-weight stretch; 4 woven; 5 fusible stitch-reinforced; 6 fusible heavy-weight.

Threads

A good-quality thread is strong and elastic with a consistent thickness. It has a smooth surface that resists tangling. Poor-quality threads, often sold in bulk packs, have a fluffy texture and tend to snap readily. Such thread is only suitable for basting.

To blend in, thread should be the same colour or slightly darker than the fabric you are working with. Lay a single thread across the fabric surface to get the best match. If the fabric has several colours in it, match the predominant colour. Try holding some lengths of thread across the fabric to see which colour blends in the best. Threads are available in a variety of fibres and thicknesses. Use the following guide to find the best thread for the job in hand.

Mercerized sewing cotton

This is a strong, smooth thread with a soft sheen for general sewing on all fabric types. It is suitable for natural or man-made fabrics.

Synthetic sewing thread

Normally made from spun polyester, this very strong, elastic thread is suitable for all general sewing. It is especially recommended for use with synthetic fabrics and any jersey or knitted fabric.

Basting thread

Basting thread is poor-quality thread used only for temporary hand stitching. It breaks easily so that the stitches can be removed quickly. Normally available in black or white, any poor-quality coloured thread can be used. Avoid using dark thread on light fabric or vice versa.

Linen thread

Linen thread is a very strong thread that is used in tailoring for sewing on buttons. Run the thread through a wax block before use.

Silk thread

Silk thread is a soft, glossy, luxury thread designed for sewing silk and wool fabrics. It has plenty of "give" and is extremely durable. Silk thread is ideal for fine hand sewing and is also used for embroidery.

Strong thread

Strong thread is used for heavy-weight fabrics where there will be strain on the seams, on items such as coats, suits and furnishings. It is also used for top-stitching and quilting. Buttonhole thread, a strong thread with a predominant twist, is used for working hand-made buttonholes.

Ensuring good results

If an outfit you have sewn doesn't quite match up to one you can buy, it could be the choice of fabric or the way you have handled it that lets it down. With such a range of exquisite fabrics on the market, there is no need for "hand-made" to mean a cheaper alternative or second-best. Staff in most dressmaking shops will be pleased to pass on their knowledge about choosing the best fabric for a particular pattern.

Preparing fabric

If you choose a fabric with a large design, you will need to position the pattern pieces very carefully when cutting out. Checked and striped fabrics work best on simple, uncomplicated shapes that allow the fabric to make a statement. Large checks and stripes can be overwhelming, so choose your pattern carefully.

In commercial pattern books some patterns are marked "unsuitable for stripes or plaids" because they probably have complicated seams that would be virtually impossible to match. As a rule, look out for paper patterns that illustrate the made-up garment or item in a fabric similar to

the one you are considering using. This should guarantee success.

Once you have chosen the fabric and pattern for your project, the temptation is to get cutting straight away. Curb your enthusiasm – a little time spent checking and preparing the fabric before you begin will help prevent costly mistakes later.

Before beginning any sewing project, it is essential to straighten the fabric. This is because when the fabric is wrapped around the bolt by the manufacturer, it can be pulled slightly out of shape, and this may not become obvious until you have already started sewing. Problems such as designs not matching, cushion covers that aren't square, curtains not hanging straight or fabric draping

incorrectly are all caused by the fabric being slightly off-grain.

It is always a good idea, therefore, to check whether your fabric is off-grain before starting any sewing project. You can do this by folding the fabric in half lengthways with the selvages together to see if the two crossways ends meet squarely.

Often, you will have to straighten the ends before you can check the grain, by tearing the fabric or pulling a thread. Sometimes it may not be obvious that the fabric is not straight because the bolt or roll was used as a guide for cutting by the store assistant – this can make the end look straight. Always check it anyway, it takes little time and will ensure good results.

Straightening fabric ends

If the fabric has an obvious weave or woven pattern such as a check, it can be cut straight easily, but you will probably have to tear or cut along a thread to guarantee a straight line.

Tearing is the quickest way to straighten a fabric end but this is only suitable for plain-weave fabrics such as calico or poplin. Try a test piece first to ensure that tearing your fabric won't ruin it each side of the tear, or cause it to suddenly tear lengthways instead. The safest way to straighten the end is by pulling a thread. It is time-consuming, but worth the effort.

1 Look carefully at the weave of the fabric and snip into the selvage next to where the first thread goes straight across. Pull one of the crossways threads until the fabric gathers up. ◀

2 Ease the gathers gently along the thread as far as possible and then cut carefully along this line. Continue this process until you have cut right across the fabric.

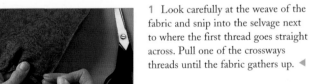

Straightening the grain

Once the end of the fabric is straight, you will be able to check if the fabric is off-grain. There are two ways to do this. You can either arrange the fabric flat on a square table or fold it in half lengthways with the selvages together. In both cases the ends should be square. If the corners don't match, the fabric needs to be straightened before you can begin cutting and sewing. If it is only slightly off-grain, the fabric can be steam-pressed into shape.

Misshapen fabric must be pulled back into shape. This can be quite hard work and for a large piece of fabric you may need to enlist the help of a friend to pull from the opposite end. This is essential and will affect the final drape of the garment or item, so don't be tempted to miss this stage.

1 Fold the fabric in half lengthways, with right sides together. Pin the raw edges together. Place upright pins into the ironing board every 13cm/5in along the selvage. Press the fabric from the selvage into the fold until the weave is absolutely straight, but avoid pressing the fold. Leave fabric to cool before removing the pins.

2 To pull fabric back into shape, hold it firmly on each side of the narrow corners and pull your hands apart. Keep moving your hands down each side, pulling firmly, until you reach the other corners. This is easier to do if two people work from opposite corners. Check to see if the corners are square then press the fabric as in step 1.

PRE-SHRINKING FABRIC

Man-made or natural fibres will shrink when washed or dry cleaned unless they have been pre-shrunk by the manufacturer. Although shrinkage of 3 per cent may appear small, bear in mind that this can result in floor-length curtains being 5–7.5cm/2–3in shorter after cleaning.

• Problems also arise in dressmaking when interfacings don't shrink to the same degree as the outer fabric, causing collars and cuffs to pucker. Quilt-makers use this puckered effect to create instant "antique" patchwork quilts by washing a quilt in hot water after it has been stitched to shrink the cotton wadding (batting).

• Shrink cotton and other washable fabrics in a washing machine, or in a basin of hot water (using no soap or detergent). Fold the fabric to fit and leave it immersed for up to an hour. Lift the fabric out and roll it up to remove the excess moisture before hanging it up by the selvage. Keep the fabric in shape with regularly spaced clothes pegs, then press it on the wrong side while still slightly damp.

• Wool fabrics need to be handled with the utmost care and should be shrunk by dry cleaning if possible. Otherwise, straighten the ends of the fabric and fold it in half crossways. Place the folded fabric in the centre of a damp sheet. Fold the edges of the sheet on to the wool fabric then roll it up carefully, keeping the sheet on the outside all the time. Leave the fabric overnight then press lightly with a steam iron.

CHECKING FOR FLAWS

Once the fabric is ready for cutting, open it out with the right side facing up and examine it carefully for flaws.

• Flaws usually occur during the manufacturing process and may not be obvious on the wrong side. Sometimes a thread snaps during the weaving or knitting process, causing a weak point or knot. Alternatively, the printing may not be perfect or there may be a dirty mark.

• If you have enough fabric, avoid the flaw, otherwise you will have to return the length to the shop or buy extra fabric.

• Some fabrics, especially pale colours and synthetics, can become quite badly soiled along the foldline while on display and will require cleaning before use.

Washing and caring for fabrics

Scientists are constantly searching for ways to make fabrics repel dirt and stay cleaner longer, but until they succeed laundry is an essential part of our lives. An average family will spend about 12 hours a week washing, ironing and putting away the clothes they wear. Laundering, although caring for the fabric by getting it clean, is liable to cause some deterioration eventually by shrinking the fabric and fading colours. To help keep these problems to a minimum all clothes are labelled with the fabric they are made from and care information for treating them.

The present care labelling system is based on five symbols: a wash tub, an iron, a circle in a square (tumble dryer), a circle (dry cleaning) and a triangle (bleaching). These five symbols are used in groups on a label to describe exactly how to clean, iron or tumble dry a garment.

Sort clothes initially according to their colour. Keep whites separate, as even pale and neutral shades will eventually cause them to look grey.

In the United States, care instructions are written on labels.

Understanding the washcare symbols

 The number inside the wash tub symbol indicates the maximum recommended Centigrade temperature you can use using a normal cycle.

 A single bar under the wash tub symbol indicates a gentler washing action. This symbol is used for synthetic fabrics.

 Two bars under the wash tub symbol indicates that the wool wash or delicate cycle should be used.

 This symbol is used for hand wash garments only. The label will give other details such as temperature, drying and ironing.

 A crossed-out wash tub indicates dry cleaning only. It is followed by another symbol giving information on the dry cleaning process to be used.

 The letter inside the circle indicates which solvents are suitable for dry cleaning the article. An "A" means that all solvents normally used for dry cleaning are suitable.

 A "P" indicates that only certain solvents are suitable. Dry cleaners are currently restricted to four suitable solvents for these articles.

 A bar under a circle indicates that the garment is sensitive to some dry cleaning processes and must be cleaned under strict conditions.

 A crossed-out circle indicates that the garment is not suitable for dry cleaning.

 This symbol indicates that the garment may be tumble dried.

 A single dot inside the tumble drying symbol means that the garment should be dried on the low heat setting.

 Two dots indicate that the garment can be dried on the high heat setting.

 A crossed-out tumble drying symbol means that the garment is not suitable for tumble drying. This symbol is usually followed by further instructions such as "dry flat".

 A tee-shirt in a square indicates that the garment should be dried flat away from direct heat. It is used for garments that can easily be pulled out of shape.

 An iron with one dot is used for synthetic fabrics that melt at low temperatures. Set the iron at its coolest setting.

Fabric terminology

Above: Wool fibres will mat together to make felt if they are roughly handled or washed in hot or boiling water.

Two dots on an iron indicate a medium heat setting. This symbol is used for wool, silk and some synthetic fibre mixtures.

Three dots indicate the hottest setting on an iron. This symbol appears on cotton, linen and man-made fibres such as viscose.

A crossed-out iron means do not iron. This usually indicates that the fabric has a special finish or embellishments which would be damaged by an iron.

A triangle is found on imported garments. It refers to chlorine bleach and not to the bleaching agents found in washing powders.

A crossed-out triangle means do not use chlorine bleach.

The success of a project depends on the correct folding and accurate placement of pattern pieces, so it is important to learn the terms commonly used in commercial patterns. Some fabrics handle very differently if cut on the crossways grain rather than on the lengthways grain, and designs or motifs can end up facing in the wrong direction. Most fabrics are cut with the right sides of the fabric together and can be folded on the lengthways or crossways fold. Nap designs have a design or surface texture that means the fabric must be folded lengthways or not at all.

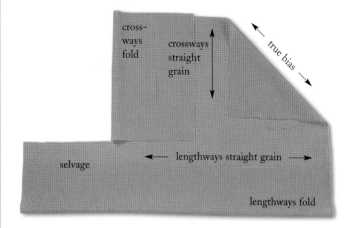

Bias

Bias is any diagonal line across woven fabric. Fabric cut on the bias has more stretch than fabric cut on the straight grain, and the most stretch is achieved on the true bias. This occurs when the selvage edge on one side is folded over to run parallel to the crossways grain. Patterns cut on the bias drape beautifully. Bias strips are used for binding or piping curved edges.

Folds

Fabric is usually sold off a roll or from a bolt (a flat cardboard base). On narrow widths the fabric is flat with a selvage at each edge, but more often the fabric is folded in half lengthways so that the selvages lie together. This fold is used for centre front seams and should be in the centre of a large design. Crossways folds are used when cutting wide pattern pieces.

Grain

Woven fabrics are made up of two sets of threads. The crossways, or weft threads go over and under the stronger warp threads that run the length of the fabric. The grain is the direction in which these threads are woven. Warp threads running parallel to the selvage are on the lengthways grain. When the weft threads run perpendicular to the selvage they are on the crossways grain.

Selvage

This is the narrow flat band running lengthways down each side of the fabric. The threads are strong and closely woven and provide a straight, ready-finished edge for centre back seams or cushion cover zipper openings. On some fabrics, such as jersey, the selvage is rather ragged and it is better to trim it off.

Cutting paper patterns

Commercial patterns usually come with a cutting guide. This tells you how to fold the fabric and arrange the pattern pieces, and is carefully worked out. You may make a mistake if you change things around. If there is no cutting plan, the following information will be useful.

Fabrics are usually folded lengthways with right sides together. This makes it easy to mark the fabric on the wrong side and allows you to sew pieces together quickly.

The straight grain line is the most important line on the pattern piece. This line is placed to follow the lengthways grain on the fabric and runs parallel to the selvages. If the grain line is inaccurately placed, the item or garment will not hang straight. Check carefully even after the pattern is pinned to the fabric.

1 Place the pattern piece lengthways on the fabric. Measure an equal distance to the selvage from each end of the pattern and insert a pin at the top and bottom.

2 Pin around the sides every 7.5–10cm/3–4in to firmly secure the pattern piece to the fabric. Refer to the tips below before cutting out.

TIPS FOR SUCCESSFUL PATTERN CUTTING

• Select the cutting guide to match the width and type of fabric and size of pattern. Draw a circle around the cutting guide you intend to use.

• Pin all the pattern pieces on to the fabric before cutting out.

• Check that the straight grain lines are parallel to the selvages and the foldlines are on the fold.

• Make sure that any alterations to the main pattern pieces have been applied to corresponding pieces such as facings.

• Cut out the pattern pieces with the printed side facing up, unless stated otherwise. This is shown as shaded in the cutting guide.

• When a pattern piece has to be repeated, draw around it with tailor's chalk, marking the notches then move it to another location.

• Sometimes a "Cut 1" pattern piece overhangs the fabric in a cutting guide. Cut all other pieces first then open out the fabric with the right side up. Pin in place, using the foldline as a guide for the straight grain.

Hold your hand flat on the pattern piece and cut the fabric with large shears, using long, even cuts. Move around the table rather than moving the fabric, keeping your hand resting on the fabric at all times so that you do not accidentally move it.

Seam allowances

Check whether seam allowances are included in the pattern pieces or if they have to be added. If required, use tailor's chalk and a ruler to add 15mm/⅝in extra for the seam allowance on all sides except for the foldlines.

1 Arrange this type of pattern piece so that the fold line lies exactly along the fold of the fabric. Pin along the fold every 7.5–10cm/3–4in, then all around the edge.

Directional fabrics

Many plain, or small-patterned fabrics can be cut out quite easily without much thought as to how the pattern pieces are laid out. Directional fabrics, on the other hand, have a textured surface or design that requires greater care when folding, positioning and cutting out.

Fabrics such as velvet, dévoré, moleskin and corduroy have a pile, and can only be cut in one direction. Hold the fabric lengthways against your body and move your hand across the surface to determine the direction of the pile. It should feel smooth when you stroke your hand up the fabric. Dress patterns and curtains are normally cut with the pile facing upwards so that the colour looks richer, but they can also be used in the other direction for a paler effect. Whatever you decide, ensure it matches throughout.

Follow the same approach for one-way prints and dyed fabrics such as ombré, which shade from top to bottom, by making all the pattern pieces face the same way. All these fabrics are known as directional or "with nap", and also include satin and brocade. They have to be treated as directional because of the way the light reflects from the surface.

The cutting guide will have a pattern layout for using "with nap"

Below: Everyday clothing and mundane checks and stripes have been pieced into an unusual patchwork quilt.

Above: Velvet has a directional nap that requires careful handling.

fabrics if the pattern is suitable. Fold the fabric lengthways with right sides together to give a smooth surface on which to pin the pattern. Don't fold directional fabric crossways before cutting because the pattern or pile on the lower layer will be facing in the opposite direction to that on the top layer. If your pattern is too wide for the lengthways fold, cut the fabric in half crossways and rotate the top piece until both layers face in the same direction.

Patterned fabrics

Most of us will probably use patterned fabric for a sewing project at least once. Small random prints can be cut out in the same way as plain fabric, but large designs, checks and stripes need to be studied closely and arranged carefully before cutting. The position of a large, bold design on the finished item can be crucial to its success.

Border designs that are positioned along the hem of garments and curtains can be difficult because the exact finished length needs to be determined before cutting. Mark the hem line on the pattern, allowing for turnings, and position the border design just above the line.

On dress patterns or cushions, any large, bold designs are usually positioned centrally. You will find this easier if you make complete pattern pieces from tracing paper before you begin. Work with the fabric in a single layer with the right side facing up, and position, for example, the front bodice pattern piece centrally on the design. Cut other corresponding pattern pieces so that the design will be at the same level on the garment.

Soft furnishings such as loose covers and curtains will look wrong if a large design is badly positioned. Plan the cutting layout, allowing extra fabric for matching seams and positioning the design.

Checks and stripes

Checks are made up of stripes arranged horizontally and vertically across the fabric to form a repeating pattern. This pattern can be even or uneven, depending on the arrangement of the stripes. Because the bold lines of a checked design should match horizontally and vertically on a garment or soft furnishing item, it is essential to test these fabrics before cutting as some fabrics that appear to be even are actually uneven.

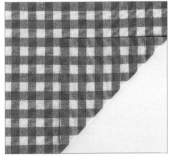

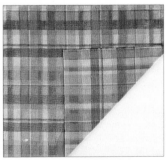

1 Turn over a corner of the fabric so that the fold lies centrally through the squares of the check design. In an even check, the line widths and colours match in both directions.

2 This check appears to be even, but when the fabric is folded on the diagonal it is obvious that the horizontal lines are stronger than the vertical lines.

3 In an uneven check, the line widths and colours may match if folded vertically or horizontally but don't match when folded diagonally.

Left: Striped fabrics work well with simple designs and are particularly associated with country-style furnishings.

Cutting even checks

Fabrics with even checks can usually be cut on the normal "without nap" pattern layout. Open the fabric out and re-fold it down the centre of the main check line.

1 Insert pins along the foldline. Work out from the centre, pinning along each main check line, making sure that both layers match exactly.

2 Place the pattern pieces so that the centre front line and back seam lines are exactly on the dominant check line. Move the pattern pieces up or down this line until the side seam notches match across the garment.

3 When making garments with front facings, make sure the notches match the corresponding pattern piece. Place sleeves with the dominant check line running down the centre of the pattern piece, and match them by placing the notch on the front sleeve head at the same level as the armhole notch on the bodice.

Cutting uneven checks

Cutting fabrics with uneven checks is not suitable for a beginner, and it is advisable to choose simple patterns to reduce the amount of matching required. Seam lines cut at an angle should have the check lines coming together as shown, but this can look very fussy if there are a lot of seams. The principle for pattern cutting is the same as for even checks, but, since the check can only be matched in one direction, use a "with nap" layout. It may also be easier to open the fabric out and cut it on a single thickness, making sure you turn the pattern pieces over to cut the left-hand side. Pin the seams carefully and baste if necessary before sewing to ensure neat, accurate matching.

Cutting striped fabrics

Striped fabrics are easier to match than checked ones because the lines run in one direction only, but the same preparation and cutting principles apply. Horizontal striped fabrics can be cut more accurately if the stripes are pinned at regular intervals. First determine the length and position the hem line along the dominant stripe. The pattern can then be matched across by placing corresponding notches on the same stripe. Facings should match the main pattern piece. Position sleeves so that the front sleeve head notch is on the same stripe as the front armhole notch. Unbalanced horizontal stripes must be cut using a "with nap" layout.

Above: Striped silk has a formal appearance, particularly when it is used on a grand scale to furnish the home.

Right: Large- and small-scale gingham checks in natural fabrics will soften with age and wear.

Fabrics requiring special handling

Although it is much easier to stitch a plain cotton fabric than a knitted velour, your dressmaking will be rather dull if you don't try some of the more unusual fabrics, such as lace, leather, fake fur or any of the sheer fabrics. There are some wonderful fabrics available today that can make a simple design exceptional and quite unique.

Lace

Lace and lacy fabrics are unique because of their loose, open construction. They can be used for the whole garment or a part such as the bodice, sleeves or skirt. Lace is normally lined on the bodice and skirt, but cut on its own for sleeves. When made in this way, lace garments are usually luxury items, since they require special laundering and care.

Lace works well with a variety of fabrics such as velvet, crêpe, satin or taffeta. Choose a pattern to suit the main fabric, with simple lines to show off the lace. When using lace with another fabric, check that both fabrics require similar laundering.

Lace is constructed differently from woven or knitted fabrics and is backed with a fine mesh. It can be cut in any direction. Look at the motifs and the pattern they create, and decide if the lace motifs can be used as a border or the hem of a garment. Lace does not fray and can be cut around the motifs to produce an attractive scallop edge.

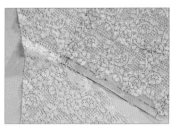

1 Position the stitching line of the pattern piece along the bottom of the lace motifs. The lace can be trimmed neatly along this line and then cut in the normal way for the other seams.

Sheer and satin fabrics

Voile, muslin, georgette, organza and batiste are sheer fabrics with quite different handling. Crisp sheers such as organza are quite easy to cut and stitch, but the softer sheers such as georgette tend to slip, requiring greater care when dressmaking. Sheer fabrics can be stitched in multiple layers to produce a moiré effect but need to be lined in certain parts to make them less transparent. Satin fabrics handle in a similar way to soft sheers when stitching. Use narrow, rolled hems and choose methods of fastening that will keep machine stitching on the right side to a minimum. Rouleaux loops and invisible or prick-stitched zippers are suitable for these fabrics.

Soft sheer fabrics and satin are quite difficult to sew. The fabric tends to shift and slide and can snag as it is stitched. Use a new needle – a ballpoint needle is often recommended because it slips between the threads without splitting them.

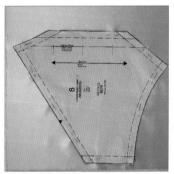

Above: Satin has a smooth, glossy appearance and is soft to the touch, making it ideal for lingerie.

1 Satin and sheer fabrics may be permanently marked by pins. Place the pins in the seam allowance.

2 On sheer fabrics, stitch the seams between two layers of tissue paper. The paper can be torn away later.

Fur fabrics

Imitation fur fabric should be treated as a pile fabric. Pin the pattern pieces with the pile going in the same direction. When cutting long-hair fabrics, use a small pair of pointed scissors to snip the fabric, leaving the pile intact on the surface.

1 Stitch a seam then ease the long hairs out of the seam, using a large, blunt needle from the right side to make it almost invisible. Excess fur can be trimmed from the seam allowance on the inside to reduce bulk.

Leather and plastic

Leather, suede and plastic fabrics such as vinyl, PVC, imitation leather and polythene shower curtain fabric can all be stitched on a domestic sewing machine. Choose simple styles with few seam lines and avoid seams that need to be eased. It is important to make sure there are no pins used outside the seam allowance. Tape and paper clips are suitable alternatives. Use the tape to fix the pattern pieces and both methods for seams.

Below: Seams on leather can be pressed on the wrong side, using a dry, medium iron.

1 Paperclips or masking tape can be used to hold leather or plastic instead of pins.

2 Use a long stitch as small stitches tear more easily and plastic especially will split along the seam line like perforated paper. Ensure that the seams are stitched correctly first time.

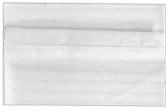

3 If seams are stitched in the wrong place on plastic or leather, they can be taken in but not let out. The previous stitches will leave an unsightly row of holes on the right side.

4 To make it easier to stitch leather or plastic, use a roller foot or place strips of tissue paper on either side of the seam to help it slip under the presser foot.

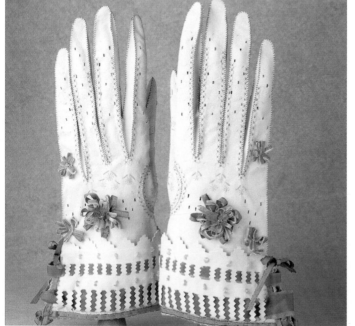

Marking up fabric

Printed pattern pieces contain information that must be transferred on to the fabric before sewing. The position of darts, centre front and centre back lines, buttonholes and seam openings are the most common, but every symbol and line you transfer will make sewing much easier.

Tailor's tacks

Tailor's tacks are threads used to mark points such as the top of darts. The symbol for a tailor tack is a dot on the pattern. They are suitable for many fabrics. Use a different colour for large and small dots on the pattern and work with a long double strand of thread without a knot.

1 Take a small stitch through the pattern and fabric. Leave a long tail. Make a second stitch on top of the first, pulling the thread through until a loop is formed.

2 To save time, work groups of tailor's tacks, leaving a long strand between each one. Snip the middle of the loops and the strands between each one.

3 Pull the layers apart gently and snip the threads between the layers, leaving short tufts on each piece. Handle the pattern pieces carefully to prevent the tufts from coming loose.

Carbon paper and tracing wheel

Use these to mark the wrong side of closely woven, hard-wearing fabrics such as PVC, plastic and leather. Use a smooth wheel for a solid line.

Dressmaker's carbon paper is available in a variety of colours. Choose a colour that will show up on the fabric without being a contrast. Try out the carbon paper on a scrap of fabric and steam press or hand wash to ensure the marks will disappear.

1 With the pattern in place, inset a carbon sheet on each side of the folded fabric, with the coloured side facing the wrong side of the fabric.

2 ◀ Using the wheel, trace along the lines to be transferred, pressing hard enough to produce a light line on both pieces of fabric. If necessary, use a ruler to keep the wheel straight. Mark dots and other symbols with a short line or cross.

Tailor's chalk and pins

Tailor's chalk is generally used for drawing around pattern pieces before cutting out, or for last-minute marking on soft-surfaced fabrics. It can be rubbed off easily, so you should baste along the chalked lines to make a more permanent mark.

1 Push a pin through the pattern and both layers of fabric at each point to be marked.

2 ◀ Peel back the tissue paper, leaving the pins in the fabric, and chalk the fabric where the pins are, joining them up if necessary.

Pinning and basting

These techniques are quick, temporary methods of joining or marking pieces of fabric. Any thread that contrasts with the fabric can be used, but avoid using dark colours on white fabric, or vice versa, as fibres will remain in the holes and leave a coloured mark. Use a long needle. Cut a length of thread long enough to sew the whole length and secure with a knot or a loose back stitch that can be easily pulled out.

Pinning for hand sewing

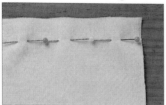

Insert pins along the seam line before basting. Arrange them in the same direction as you sew to avoid pricking your finger and only remove pins as you reach them. Use as many pins as required to hold the fabrics together. You will need more on a curved or gathered edge.

Uneven basting

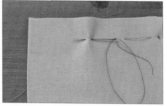

Basting is used on seam lines to hold two layers of fabric together, or for marking guidelines such as the centre front of a garment. You can also use basting to attach lining or interfacings to the main fabric, or to baste a hem before sewing it in place.

Strong basting

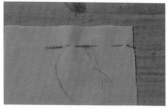

Use this stitch where there will be a lot of strain on the seam during construction or fitting. Work a back stitch every few basting stitches. Strong basting is ideal for holding together two different textures such as a satin lining and wool.

Pinning for machine sewing

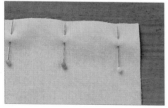

If you intend to sew by machine without basting, insert pins across the seam line. Stitch slowly over the pins and the needle will slip over each without bending. Insert pins across the seam line when easing or gathering fabric before basting. Insert the pins up or down, depending on whether you are left- or right-handed, so that you can remove them easily as you stitch over them.

Slip basting

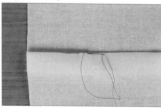

Use this from the right side of the fabric for final fitting adjustments or to ensure perfect matching of checks, stripes and patterns. Fold under the seam on one side and crease. Place the folded edge on the seam line of the other piece, matching the design carefully, and pin. Take small stitches alternately through the fold, then through the other piece. Slip basting looks like even basting if the seam is opened out for sewing.

Diagonal basting

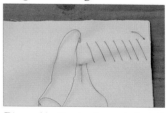

Diagonal basting is a large stitch used to insert interfacing and hold linings and facings in place. Work the stitch on a flat surface unless you are using it to hold the roll line on collars and lapels. Take small straight stitches through the fabric at right angles to the edge, forming long diagonal stitches on the top and short parallel stitches on the underside. Don't pull the thread tight or ridges will form.

Sewing by hand

In the days before sewing machines, every garment, curtain or furnishing item was sewn by hand. It seems miraculous now that so much was achieved, often in poor light. Sewing machines have, without doubt, taken the drudgery out of sewing but they cannot entirely replace hand sewing. Hand sewing should not be hurried as the quality of your stitches will affect the finished appearance of the project.

Beginning a hand stitch

Hand-sewn stitches are normally worked in thread that closely matches the fabric colour and fibre content. Work in good light, either close to a window or with an angled lamp. Use a short length of thread and a short fine needle to suit the fabric you are using.

1 Pull a length of thread from the reel no longer than the distance between your elbow and wrist. Cut the thread at an angle to make it easier to feed through the eye of the needle. Pull the cut end through the eye to about three-quarters of its length.

2 Wind the end of the thread once around your forefinger about 12mm/ ½in from the tip and hold it in place with your thumb. Rub your finger down your thumb until the threads form a twisted loop. Slide your finger and thumb down the thread to tighten the loop and form a small knot. On fine or see-through fabric where a knot would show, use a small double back stitch.

3 Take the first stitch on the wrong side, preferably hidden in a seam or fold.

Finishing off

Finish with a knot or several back stitches, one on top of the other, on the wrong side, ideally hidden in a seam or fold. If you are using back stitches, weave the thread in and out before cutting off. The finishing knot is flatter than a beginning knot.

1 Make a loop by taking a tiny back stitch on the wrong side. Take the needle through the loop and pull through until a second loop forms.

2 Finally take the needle back through the second loop and pull tight. Snip off the long end.

Hand stitches

Hand stitches are used where machine sewing is awkward or undesirable. There are many types of stitch for particular uses.

Running stitch

This basic stitch is used for gathering, smocking and quilting. Make several small even stitches at a time, weaving the needle in and out of the fabric at regular intervals. Use longer stitches for gathering and leave the thread end loose for pulling up.

Back stitch

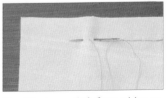

Use this strong stitch for repairing or sewing lengths of seam that are difficult to reach by machine. Bring the needle up through the fabric on the seam line. Take a small stitch back along the seam and bring the needle out an equal distance in front of where the thread last emerged.

Half back stitch

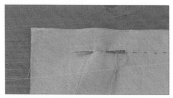

Half back stitch is suitable for stitching seams or inserting sleeves by hand. The small stitches are more attractive and stronger than ordinary back stitch. Half back stitch is also used on facings to prevent the edge from showing on the right side of the garment. Work this stitch in the same way as back stitch but take only a half stitch back and a whole stitch forward. This forms small even stitches on the top side and long overlapping stitches on the underside.

Slip stitch

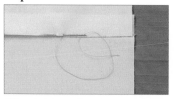

Slip stitch is used to close gaps, attach pockets and insert linings. A variation of it known as slip hemming is used to sew hems. When worked neatly, it is an almost invisible stitch. Take a small stitch through the fold then another through the fabric underneath. Make the stitches the same length and keep the thread straight. Pull the thread taut without causing the fabric to pucker. Slip hemming is worked in the same way but only a tiny stitch is taken through the underneath fabric.

Oversewing

Oversewing is used to hold two folded edges together. It is more visible, but also much stronger, than slip stitching. Work with the two folds held together in your hand. Take a tiny stitch straight through both folds, if possible catching only one thread. Continue along the folds, making a row of very small slanting stitches on the right side. In traditional patchwork, the oversewing which holds patches together is worked from the wrong side.

Prick stitch

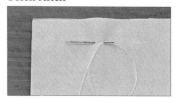

Prick stitch is an almost invisible stitch. It is used to insert zippers in fine or sheer fabrics, and to sew layers of fabrics together from the right side where a row of machine stitching would be too stiff or unsightly. Work in the same way as half back stitch, but take the needle back over only one or two threads each time to form a row of tiny surface stitches with longer reinforcing stitches on the wrong side.

Hem stitch

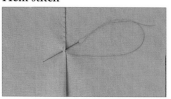

This is a diagonal stitch worked to hold down a fold of fabric such as a binding. Despite its name, it is not suitable for hemming a garment or curtains because it shows on the right side. Hem stitch can be worked into a row of machine stitching to finish cuffs or a waistband on the inside. Take a tiny stitch through the fabric and diagonally up through the edge of the fold at the same time. Continue in this way, keeping the stitches 3–5mm/$^{1}/_{8}$–$^{1}/_{4}$in apart, depending on the fabric thickness.

Blanket stitch

Traditionally used to neaten the raw edges of woollen blankets, this stitch is quick to work and ideal for preventing fabric from fraying while working embroidery. It can be used as a decorative stitch and also for appliqué. Secure your first stitch at the edge of the fabric, and then work from left to right with the edge towards you. Insert the needle through the right side about 5mm/$^{1}/_{4}$in from the edge. Bring the needle back out over the thread loop and pull it taut. Continue working evenly spaced stitches in this way to add an edge to the fabric.

Sewing by machine

Few people would even think of beginning a sewing project without a sewing machine. Sewing by machine is quick and, if the tension has been set correctly, extremely neat. Machine stitching is indispensable when sewing long straight seams in soft furnishings and produces strong seams in dressmaking. Use machine stitching in conjunction with hand sewing for the most professional results.

Sewing a seam

One of the first tasks in any sewing project is stitching a seam. Most soft furnishing and dressmaking patterns use a 15mm/⅝in seam allowance – any alteration will affect the final fit.

1 Baste or pin the seam across the seam line, with the right sides of the fabric together. This will hold the fabric together while you sew.

2 Place the fabric under the presser foot so that the edge of the seam is next to the 15mm/⅝in line on the needle plate and the fabric is 5mm/¼in behind the needle. Use the hand wheel to take the needle down into the fabric, then begin to sew.

3 Sew at a speed that is comfortable for you, guiding the fabric along the 15mm/⅝in line on the needle plate.

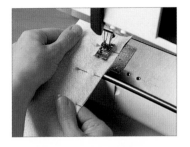

Turning corners and sewing curves

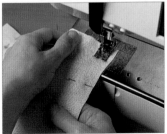

Removing stitches

1 Stitch down the first length, leaving a 15mm/⅝in seam allowance. Slow down as you approach the corner and work the last few stitches by turning the hand wheel. Stop 15mm/⅝in from the edge with the needle in the fabric. Lift the presser foot and swing the fabric around until the next seam is lined up with the guideline on the needle plate. Lower the foot and continue sewing. You may have to turn the fabric back and take another stitch or two until the edge is exactly on the 15mm/⅝in line on the needle plate.

2 Sew slowly around soft curves, keeping the edge of the fabric opposite the presser foot on the guideline of the needle plate. On tighter curves, stop and turn the fabric slightly into the curve before beginning. Keep stopping every few stitches to adjust the line of the fabric until the curve is complete. To ensure that two curves are exactly the same, for example on a collar, make a template of the shape along the sewing line and cut out. Mark the second curve along the seam line before sewing.

1 Unless the fabric is fine or delicate, the easiest way to remove stitches is by using a seam ripper. Slip the point underneath a stitch and cut it against the sharp curved edge of the tool. Cut every two or three stitches, then turn the fabric over and pull the reverse-side thread out. Brush the loose threads from the right side of the fabric and steam press to close the holes. You can run the seam ripper up the seam to rip stitches, but you risk cutting the fabric. On fine or delicate fabrics, lift and cut the stitches one at a time.

Machine stitches

The type of machine you have will determine the range of stitches at your disposal. The stitches listed here are the ones most commonly used in general sewing. Check your handbook for the range of stitches possible on your machine. Try out a stitch on a double scrap of fabric before you start.

Overlocking

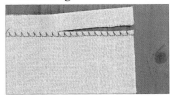

Overlocking is worked directly over the edge of the fabric, stitching and finishing the seam in one. Alternatively, stitch along the seam line then trim, as shown above.

Satin stitch

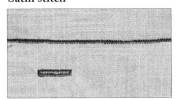

Satin stitch is a zigzag with the stitch length set almost at zero. It is used for buttonholes and machine appliqué. Use a clear-view foot to allow enough room for the bulky stitch underneath. Satin stitch can make the fabric gather if the stitches are too wide, so check that the stitch width is right for the fabric before you start. Buttonholes consist of two parallel rows of narrow satin stitches with a few double-width stitches at each end to finish.

Straight stitch

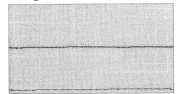

This is the stitch most widely used to join two pieces of fabric together. For ordinary fabric set the stitch length dial between 2 and 3. If the fabric is very fine or heavy, alter the stitch length to suit: use a shorter stitch for fine fabrics and a longer one for heavy fabrics. If you have an automatic sewing machine you can work a stretch straight stitch, which is useful for sewing fabrics such as jersey. Quick basting stitches can be worked by machine. Use the longest straight stitch possible to make it easy to pull out the thread at a later stage.

Blind-hemming (blindstitching)

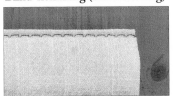

To work this stitch, a blind hemming (blind stitching) foot must be attached first. This stitch is suitable for heavy or bulky fabrics where the stitch won't show on the right side. The hem is basted and then fed under the foot, and is sewn with a series of straight stitches followed by a zigzag stitch which picks up the main fabric. Adjust the zigzag to make the stitch into the fold as small as possible.

Zigzag

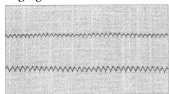

Zigzag stitches are used for finishing edges, for machine appliqué and as decoration. Try different lengths and widths of stitch to find which one suits the fabric best. In general, the stitch should be as small and narrow as possible. Wider versions of zigzag such as triple zigzag and herringbone stitch are useful for sewing elastic on to fabric. Triple zigzag can be used for finishing seams on soft or fine fabrics. Both stitches can be used to prevent the edges of towelling (terrycloth) or knitted fabrics from curling before sewing.

Machine embroidery stitches

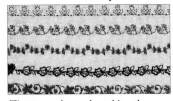

The most advanced machines have a silicone chip to create a huge range of decorative stitches which can be selected at the touch of a button. These stitches take time to stitch as the fabric moves in a circular motion to create the pattern, but the results are very effective. Automatic machines have a smaller range of stitches based on satin stitch.

Sewing seams

Seams are a crucial part of any sewing project. The perfect seam joins two pieces of fabric without puckering or stretching, and lies or hangs exactly as expected. If the seam isn't right, it is better to unpick and re-stitch it than to continue, as a poor seam will spoil the end result.

Before deciding what sort of seam to sew, think about the type of fabric and the amount of strain and wear the seam will take. The main types of seams and their special uses are shown here.

Seams can be neatened in a number of different ways to prevent them from fraying and becoming weakened, although this is not necessary if they are enclosed by fabric or a lining.

Sew angled fabric pieces in the direction of the grain rather than against it. Generally, this is from the wide end of the pattern piece to the narrow end. If you run your finger along the edge of the fabric with the grain the threads will smooth down, but they will fray if against the grain.

Plain seam

This functional seam is the basis of nearly all other seams. Use a 15mm/⅝in seam allowance. Press along the stitch line to "set" the stitches into the fabric before pressing the seam open. This seam can be worked in a narrow zigzag stitch, or with the stretch stitch on automatic machines to prevent it from splitting on knitted or stretch fabrics.

Understitching

Understitching is used to prevent an armhole or neck facing rolling out on to the right side of the garment. Grade and notch the curve. Press the seam allowances towards the facing. Work a row of small back stitches along the right side of the facing, catching the seam in at the back. Understitching can also be worked by machine.

Taping

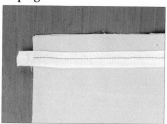

Taping strengthens a seam and prevents it from stretching out of shape. It is often used on shoulder seams and waist lines. Use a woven seam tape and baste it in place along the seam line so that it overlaps slightly into the seam allowance before stitching the seam as normal.

Plain turned-under seam

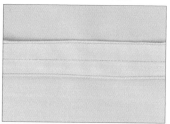

Finish off seams on light-weight, closely woven fabrics by turning under 5mm/¼in down each edge of the seam and pressing. Machine straight stitch close to the folded edge, stitching through the seam allowance only.

Plain bound seam

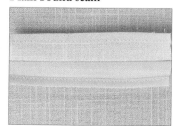

On bulky fabrics that tend to fray, for example, unlined jackets or coats, enclose the edges of the seam allowance with seam binding for a neat finish. Seam binding is slightly wider on one side and this should be underneath. Baste the seam binding in place and machine stitch as shown.

Self-bound seam

A self-bound seam is used to enclose the raw edges of light-weight fabrics and looks a little like a French seam once complete. It is the ideal way to finish the inside bottom edge of a yoke (shoulder) and useful when one side of the seam is gathered.

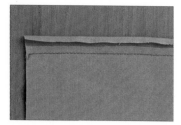

1 Trim one side of the seam allowance to 3–5mm/¹/₈–¹/₄in. Press over the edge of the seam allowance.

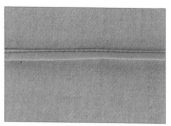

2 Fold the pressed edge over to the machine stitching and baste. Machine stitch close to the fold or hem into the machine stitching.

French seam

A French seam is used on fine, sheer fabrics and gives a beautiful straight finish. It is ideal for silk blouses, christening robes or lingerie. Unlike other seams, begin a French seam by pinning the wrong sides of the fabric together.

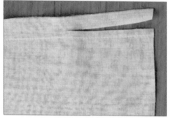

1 Stitch the wrong sides of the fabric together, 9mm/³/₈in from the seam allowance. Trim this seam to 4mm/³/₁₆in. Press the seam open.

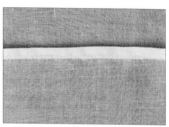

2 Fold the fabric over with right sides together, enclosing the raw edges. Press the edge flat and stitch along the seam line, 5mm/¹/₄in from the edge. Press the seam to one side.

Mock French seam

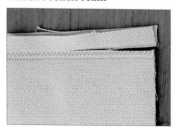

This seam looks like a French seam from the right side. It is suitable for heavy-weight fabrics or curved seams in sheer and light-weight fabrics. With right sides together, stitch a plain seam 15mm/⁵/₈in from the edge. Then machine zigzag both layers of the seam allowance together close to the seam and trim.

Plain zigzag seam

A zigzag stitch provides a quick method of finishing the raw edges of a plain seam. It can be used successfully on quite bulky fabrics. It is not a particularly neat finish and is generally used where it will not be seen. Zigzag stitch part way into the seam allowance and trim close to the stitching.

Stretch seam

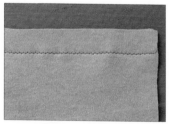

A stretch seam is worked either with a very narrow zigzag, or using the stretch stitch on an automatic machine. It is used to stitch jersey fabrics or other fabrics that have a high degree of stretch. The stitching "gives" with the fabric and prevents the seam from bursting open.

Trimming a plain seam

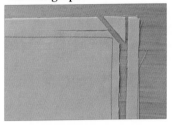

Only trim a plain seam when you are enclosing it with fabric and you need to reduce its bulk, for example, before turning a collar through. Trim the seam to 5mm/¹/₄in and cut the corners diagonally close to the stitching.

Grading a seam

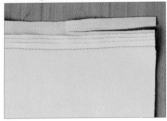

When more than two layers of fabric are joined together, the seams must be graded to reduce bulk. Trim each layer closer to the stitching as shown, making the deepest layer next to the right side of the garment. The trimmed seam allowances can be narrower on enclosed pattern pieces.

Plain pinked seam

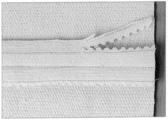

For a quick method of finishing seams on fabric that doesn't unravel, cut the edge of the seam allowance with pinking shears. This is not a very secure seam finish but can be strengthened with a row of machine stitching 5mm/¹/₄in inside the pinked edge.

Clipping curves

A curved seam needs to be snipped at regular intervals to allow it to lie flat when it is turned through. If the fabric is bulky, the seams should be graded first.

1 On inward-facing seams, snip into the fabric to within a few threads of the stitching at 1–2.5cm/¹/₂–1in intervals, depending on the curve.

2 On outward-facing curves cut small notches out of the seam at 1–2.5cm/¹/₂–1in intervals. Cut more notches when the curve is sharp.

Decorative seams

Most seams are meant to be barely noticeable on the right side of the fabric, but sometimes a more decorative seam finish is required, for example in sports and casual wear.

Lapped seam

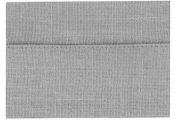

Use this seam on fabric that can be pressed into a neat fold. Turn under and press the overlapping piece of fabric along the seam line. Working from the right side, pin the folded edge along the seam line of the other fabric piece. Stitch close to the fold.

Tucked seam

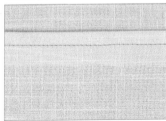

A tucked seam has a flap on the right side. Baste a 15mm/⁵/₈in plain seam and press the seam allowances to one side. On the right side, stitch 5mm/¹/₄in away from the seam through all layers, using contrasting thread if desired. Remove the basting.

Welt seam

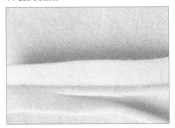 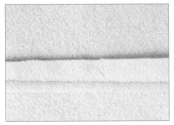 

A welt seam is similar to a top-stitched seam. It is worked on straight seams in non-fray fabrics. It is a fairly flat seam even on bulky fabrics because one seam allowance layer is trimmed. Stitch a plain seam and open out. Trim one side of the seam allowance to 5mm/¼in.

1 Press the seam allowances to one side to hide the trimmed edge. Machine stitch through the top fabric and seam allowance, enclosing the trimmed edge inside.

2 From the right side, the seam looks like a top-stitched seam. If the fabric has a lot of "give", use a stretch stitch throughout.

Flat fell seam

A flat fell seam is the classic seam used on denim jeans and casual trousers to give the distinctive double row of stitches on the right side. On reversible garments, slip stitch the inside seam allowance in place.

1 With wrong sides together, stitch a plain seam and open out the seam allowance. Trim one side of the seam allowance to 3mm/⅛in.

2 Turn under the other seam allowance and fold over the trimmed side. Baste in place and stitch through all layers close to the fold.

Slot seam

A slot seam has two tucks facing, with a piece of fabric showing behind. This seam looks particularly effective when two contrasting fabrics are used.

You can make the slot very narrow or quite wide to create a contrast panel on the garment, in which case use a wider strip in step 2.

1 With right sides together, baste a plain seam. Press open.

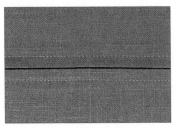 

2 Cut a strip of fabric slightly wider than the seam allowances. Baste in place over the seam on the wrong side.

3 On the right side, top stitch the same distance away from the seam line down both sides. Remove the basting thread.

Making and using bias binding

Bias binding is used to enclose raw edges along seams on the wrong side or around the edge of a neckline or armhole in place of a facing. It consists of a strip of fabric cut across the diagonal to give it stretch. You can buy pre-folded bias binding in various widths or make your own.

Making bias binding

Use a fabric of similar or lighter weight than the main fabric such as a closely woven cotton fabric with a crisp finish. For standard 12mm/½in binding, cut strips 4cm/1½in wide.

Binding an edge

Before using bias binding, steam press the strip to remove some of the slack. If the binding is going around a curved edge, turn under 5mm/¼in down each long side. Press, then fold the strip in half lengthways. Steam press into a soft curve. Open out before use and stitch along the pressed line.

You can buy a small tool that turns under the edges ready for use.

1 Fold the fabric over in one corner to form a diagonal at 45° to the selvage and cut along the fold. Mark strips of fabric four times the width of the finished binding plus a 5–9mm/¼–⅜in allowance, depending on the fabric thickness. Cut along the lines.

1 Pin the bias binding so that the seam line on the bias binding follows the seam line on the main fabric. Baste 5mm/¼in away from the raw edge of the bias strip.

2 Machine stitch next to the basting line and then trim the main fabric so that it is slightly narrower than the binding seam. Press the binding away from the main fabric.

2 With right sides together, overlap two ends at right angles. Stitch across the diagonal corner and press open. Trim the seam allowance flush with the bias binding. Join extra pieces as required.

3 Turn under 5mm/¼in and fold over to the wrong side. Pin and baste the binding in place.

4 Secure the binding with tiny hem stitches. For extra strength, work the stitches into the machine stitching.

Decorative piping

As well as providing a decorative feature on clothes and soft furnishings, piping also strengthens a seam and can protect the edge from wear. It is made by wrapping a bias strip of fabric around piping cord and enclosing it within a seam. You can use either a matching or a contrasting fabric, but it must be the same or a lighter weight than the main fabric.

Using piping cord

Piping cord is available in several widths to suit a range of different fabrics. Wrap fabric around several sizes of piping cord to check which one looks best. A lighter-weight fabric usually looks better with thin piping cord.

Piped seams are often used as a decorative feature in soft furnishings or on suits and jackets. A softer piped seam can be made without any cord.

Below and below right: Piping provides an ideal opportunity to introduce accent colours to your design. The design on the right uses a contrasting fabric type.

1 Wrap a piece of bias fabric around the cord and add a 3cm/1¼in seam allowance to each side. Cut as many bias strips as you need to that width, and steam press them to remove the excess stretch. Wrap the bias strip around the cord and pin. Stitch close to the cord, using a zipper foot.

2 Pin the piping to one piece of the main fabric, matching the raw edges, and stitch close to the previous stitching. Pin the second piece of fabric on top, matching the raw edges, and stitch through all layers as close to the piping cord as possible.

Making perfect hems

A hem adds weight to a garment or curtain and helps it to hang correctly. It is usually the last thing to be sewn, and the fabric and style influence the kind of hem and its depth. A perfect hem looks absolutely level and, if hand stitched, is almost invisible from the right side.

Measuring up

A normal hem allowance is 7.5cm/3in but for narrow hems on a full circle, bias or stretchy garments it can be as little as 3mm–2.5cm/¹⁄₈–1in. These should be hung for 24 hours before marking the hem line. Reduce excess fullness evenly and keep the stitches loose to prevent ridges forming.

Mark the hem at the final fitting when all other adjustments have been made. Put on any clothes that will be worn with the garment for the fitting.

1 Use a floor-standing hem rule and insert pins horizontally at the same height all the way around the garment to mark the bottom line. Some garments such as full skirts and trousers may look better if the hem slopes slightly to the back. Make this adjustment gradually so that it is not noticeable. Turn the hem up to the inside of the garment along the pin line.

2 Baste along the foldline, removing the pins as you go.

3 Measure and mark the depth of hem required and then trim off the excess fabric.

PREPARING A HEM

Follow these preparation steps for successful hemming, whatever hem you are sewing.

• Baste along the marked hem line and remove the pins.

• Measure the depth of hem required, allowing for turnings. Mark with pins and trim.

• Trim the seam allowances below the basting line of the hem to 5mm/¼in.

• Turn the hem up along the basted line and baste again to secure the fold.

• Ease fullness in the hem evenly around the entire garment.

Zigzag or overcast hem

This hem lies flat because there are no turnings. It creates a very smooth finish on the right side and is suitable for most weights of fabric. The raw edge can be zigzagged or overcast. Baste along the hem just below the zigzag, easing in any fullness as you go. Turn over the top edge and hold it down with your thumb then slip stitch the hem to the main garment. Work two small running stitches in the hem and take a tiny stitch into the main garment. Continue around the hem, keeping the stitches loose. Press the hem from the wrong side.

Plain turned-under hem

This hem is suitable for light- and medium-weight washable fabrics. It must be pressed from the wrong side, otherwise a ridge will form on the right side. Turn under 5mm/¹⁄₄in along the raw edge and machine stitch close to the fold. Slip hem, sliding the needle along the fold and taking a tiny stitch into the main fabric.

Seam binding

Seam binding is added to fabrics that fray easily before turning up the hem. The binding is much thinner than the main fabric and makes a neat hem finish. Seam binding is often used on trousers to protect the hem from being caught on a shoe. On the right side, machine stitch the seam binding about 5mm/¼in from the raw edge of the main fabric. Turn the hem up to the required length and baste. Hem the seam binding to the main fabric.

Machine-stitched hem

A machine-stitched hem is visible from the right side of the garment. It is suitable for knitted fabrics and on garments where top stitching is a feature, such as a shirt or unlined jacket. To create a design, machine stitch along the bottom fold as well. Baste the hem in position and ease any fullness evenly as you work. It may help to press the hem from the wrong side before machine stitching.

Hand-rolled hem

A hand-rolled hem is a delicate, soft finish for lingerie and other projects using silk or sheer fabrics. It is often used to finish the edges of silk scarves. It is quite time-consuming but well worth the effort. Machine stitch 5mm/¼in from the hem line. Trim the hem allowance close to the stitching. Roll the raw edge to enclose the machine stitching then slip stitch, catching a single thread at each stitch.

Double hem

A double hem is similar to a narrow hem but is used when the fabric is transparent. The turning is the same width as the hem itself so that no raw edge is visible through the layers of fabric. It is used for the edges of sheer curtains or for sheer fabrics such as cotton organdie. Mark the hem length and then decide on the depth of the finished hem. Cut the hem allowance twice the depth of the finished hem. Fold the hem allowance in half so that the raw edge lies along the hem line. Fold the hem up and pin or baste in place. Machine stitch or slip stitch.

Narrow hem

A narrow hem is suitable for light-weight fabrics on blouses, shirts and lingerie. The edge can be machine stitched or slip stitched. Turn under 5mm/¼in along the raw edge and turn up a narrow hem. Slip stitch along the fold. This type of hem can be worked along a gentle curve if it is eased carefully.

Machine-rolled hem

A machine-rolled hem is much stiffer than a hand-rolled hem because it has two rows of machine stitching. Use it on crisp, fine fabrics such as cotton lawn. Turn under 5mm/¼in and machine stitch along the fold. Turn under an additional 5mm/¼in and machine stitch through all the layers of the hem.

Tucks, pleats, darts and gathers

In dressmaking, flat fabric is stitched together to fit the curves of the body. To some extent pattern pieces are curved and shaped, but further shaping is usually needed to create a three-dimensional garment. The method chosen to control fullness and manipulate the fabric is very much part of the overall design. Darts, tucks and pleats control the fabric in a precise way, while gathers and shirring create a softer effect.

Tucks

These are narrow folds of fabric that are stitched to produce a decorative effect. The basic technique is the same for all tucks but the width, spacing and length can be varied to create different effects. Tucks are always worked on the straight grain. They can be narrow or wide, touching or spaced, and stitched either all the way down or only part way down for fullness. When adding tucks to a garment, for example on a plain sleeve or yoke (shoulder), work the tucks in the fabric before cutting out the pattern piece.

1 Decide on the width and spacing of the tucks. Cut a piece of paper to use as a guide to make the gauge. Mark the foldline of the tuck and the stitching lines down both edges of the fabric.

2 Draw a single thread from the fabric down the foldline of each tuck. Fold the fabric along the pulled thread lines and press. You can press the tucks without drawing a thread, but it is more difficult to keep the tuck exactly on the straight grain.

Above: These tucks are worked in a circular motion, first stitching one way, then the other, to produce a wave-like effect.

3 Baste the tucks along each stitching line. Use the gauge as a guide if the weave of the fabric is too fine. Place the basted fold under the presser foot. Use the edge of the presser foot or needle plate guide to gauge the width of the tuck and stitch parallel to the foldline. Press along each stitch line and then press the tucks to one side. Press the entire tucked area from the wrong side.

Above: Using the Cathedral Windows patchwork technique, one fabric is inset to another. The edges of the lower fabric are rolled over the inset fabric and hand stitched in place.

Pin tucks

Pin tucks are very narrow tucks, often used on baby clothes or blouses. The tucks can be stitched in the same way as spaced tucks but it is quite difficult to stitch neatly so close to the fold. For the best result, insert a twin needle in the sewing machine and thread up with two reels of thread. The upper tension can be loosened slightly to make the tucks more pronounced. Use the side of the presser foot as a guide to space the tucks.

Spaced tucks

Spaced tucks have a fixed space between each tuck. The width and spacing of the tucks should be worked out carefully to produce a balanced appearance.

Top right and right: Calico has been folded, pleated, tucked and manipulated in different ways to create interesting surface textures.

Released tucks

Released tucks are blind or spaced tucks that are only stitched part way along the length, allowing the fabric to open out at one or both ends. The fabric at the end of the tuck is never pressed and falls in soft folds to create fullness. Released tucks are often worked with the fold on the wrong side.

Blind tucks

On blind tucks the distance on the gauge between the fold, stitching line and the space between are the same, so that the fold of each tuck touches the machine stitching.

Scalloped tucks

Scalloped tucks are blind or spaced tucks that are stitched by hand to create a pretty shell effect. Soft delicate fabrics are most suitable for this type of tuck. The tucks can be stitched entirely by hand, or stitched by machine and scalloped by hand. Baste the tuck and machine stitch then mark every 9mm/^{3}/$_8$in along the stitched line. Slip a threaded needle through the tuck to the first mark. Sew two tight stitches over the tuck then slip the needle through the tuck to the next mark.

Crossed tucks

Crossed tucks are always worked before the pattern is cut out. Measure and stitch the spaced tucks in one direction first and press very carefully. Measure the tucks at right angles to the first set and baste. Machine stitch with the first tuck folds facing downwards, so that the presser foot slips over each tuck. Place the pattern piece with the horizontal tucks facing towards the bottom, and the straight grain running along one of the vertical tucks. Cut out and stay stitch the edges of the pattern piece to keep the tucks flat while making up.

Pleats

Pleats are folds in fabric that provide controlled fullness in a garment, for example on a skirt. They are usually stitched part way down the length and then pressed flat. Perfect pleats hang closed while the wearer is standing still but open to allow freedom of movement. Whether it is a small kick pleat at the back of a dress or a skirt pleated all the way around, it is necessary to be very precise during the making. Transfer all markings carefully and baste

down the entire length of a pleat before stitching. Choose fabrics carefully for a pleated garment. They should be of light to medium weight and hold a crease when pressed. Suitable fabrics include wool and wool blends, linen-mix fabric, heavier silks and some synthetic or man-made fabrics. Choose a pattern for a pleated skirt by the hip measurement rather than the waist measurement because it is easier to alter the waist line.

Marking pleats

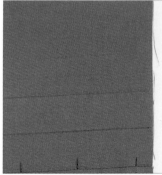

Successful pleats depend on accurate marking of the three pleat line indicators. Pleats that are left unpressed have a roll line and pleats that are pressed into a flat crease have a foldline. Both pleats also have a placement line; the roll or foldline is brought up to this line and stitched.

Pleats can be stitched either from the wrong side or top stitched on the right side. Pressed and unpressed pleats are made in the same way; it is the final pressing that makes the difference. Leave the basting thread holding the pleats closed in place until the garment is complete.

Knife pleat

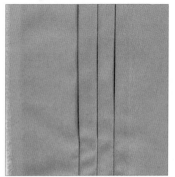

This basic pleat is a double fold of fabric pressed flat. Knife pleats all face in the same direction in a garment.

Box pleat

A box pleat is created from two knife pleats. The underneath folds meet on the wrong side.

Inverted pleat

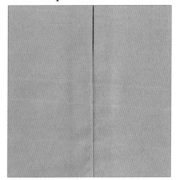

An inverted pleat is the opposite of a box pleat. The two knife pleats face each other and meet in the centre on the right side of the fabric.

Accordion pleat

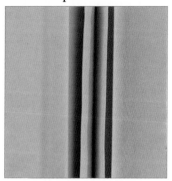

Accordion pleats lie partly open during wear. The pleats are normally permanently pressed in alternate "valley" and "mountain" folds.

Working from the wrong side

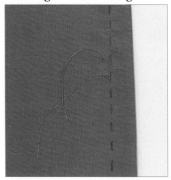

1 Mark pleat lines with basting thread or dressmaker's carbon on the wrong side of the fabric. Fold the fabric right sides together and baste along the full length of the pleat, matching fold and placement lines.

2 Mark the length of the stitched pleat and stitch down to this line. Reverse back along the line for several stitches for strength. Take out the basting thread in the stitched area only and press the pleats flat.

Removing excess bulk

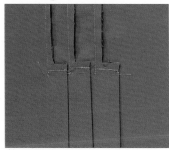

Pleats can be trimmed on the wrong side to remove excess bulk, especially around the waist line. Lift each pleat away from the main fabric on the wrong side and stitch crossways at the end of the pleat stitching. Baste along these stitch lines to hold the pleats in position. Trim the fabric above the line, leaving a 15mm/⅝in seam.

Working from the right side

1 Mark pleat lines with basting thread on the right side of the fabric. Bring the foldline up to the placement line and pin, then baste along the whole length of the pleat.

2 Mark the length of the stitched pleat and stitch down to this line. Take the thread ends to the wrong side and sew in securely.

Fitting pleated garments

Minor adjustments to pleated items can be made at the side seams but for a larger alteration make small adjustments to the top of each pleat. Divide the number of pleats by the alteration required and add or take that measurement from each pleat. If your garment has four pleats, 2.5cm/1in can be added or removed by moving the foldline of each pleat just 5mm/¼in.

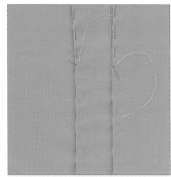

1 From the wrong side, enlarge a garment by moving the seam line into the seam allowance slightly. Reduce the garment by moving the seam allowance into the main fabric.

2 From the right side, enlarge a garment by moving the foldline over the placement line. Reduce the garment by moving the foldline back from the placement line.

Pleats with separate underlay

Some pleats have a separate underlay. Form the pleat from an extra wide seam allowance. Working from the wrong side, baste the pleat foldlines with right sides together. Stitch, then press open. Stitch the underlay in place. Tidy the raw edges. Baste the top of the underlay to hold it in place.

Darts

Darts are one of the basic dress-making techniques. It is essential to check the position of the darts on a garment before cutting out because the angle and length of each dart is crucial to the final fit and appearance.

Darts should point towards the fullest part of the body, for example the point of the bust or hip bone. If necessary, re-draw the dart, beginning about 2.5–4cm/1–1½in away from the new point. Keep the base of the dart

the same size and join the lines in a similar shape to the original.

When fitting patterns or garments, always wear the correct underwear and the shoes that will be worn with the finished item.

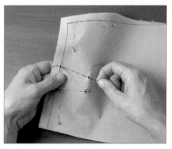

1 Mark darts by inserting a tailor's tack at each of the large dots on the pattern piece. If the outside lines of a dart are curved, it is advisable to mark along the lines as well. Darts can also be marked using dressmaker's carbon or tailor's chalk.

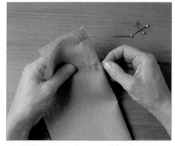

2 Pull the two layers of fabric slightly apart and snip the tailor's tacks. With right sides together, fold the dart along the centre and match the tailor's tacks. Insert pins across the dart and baste between the tailor's tacks.

3 Machine stitch the dart from the widest part, tapering to a point. Stitch inside the basting thread and work the last few stitches along the fold. Tie the ends of the thread together rather than reversing, as this can cause an unsightly bump.

4 Press along the stitch line to set the stitches, then press vertical darts towards the centre of the garment or press horizontal darts downwards. Press from the wrong side, using the tip of the iron to shape the point end of the dart. Slip a strip of brown paper under the dart before pressing to prevent an impression forming on the right side.

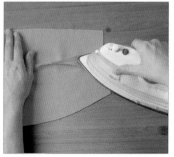

5 Deep darts or those worked in heavier fabrics can be slashed and pressed flat to reduce the bulk. Cut the dart along the foldline as far as possible and open out. This method is only suitable for lined garments where the raw edges won't fray.

6 Darts in sheer fabrics can be trimmed to make them less conspicuous from the right side. Press the dart flat and trim, leaving 5mm/¼in outside the stitches. Overcast the raw edges and press the dart to one side.

Gathers

Work gathers by hand or machine. Use gathering to ease fabric into a waistline, yoke (shoulder) or cuff.

The width of fabric is determined by the weight of the fabric and the amount of fullness required in the finished garment. If the fabric is very wide, work the gathering stitches in batches to prevent the thread snapping as it is pulled up. Insert pins between the batches of stitches for securing the thread ends.

Machine gathers pull up easily if the top tension is loosened slightly before stitching with a long stitch. Use a strong thread, such as nylon or quilting thread, in the bobbin to prevent the thread from snapping.

1 Sew the gathering threads on to the fabric. If you are hand sewing, work two parallel rows of small running stitches across the fabric on each side of the seam line. Try to keep the stitches and spacing the same size on both rows.

2 Place the two pattern pieces together with right sides facing. Pin at both ends and wrap the ends of the thread around the pin in a figure-of-eight to secure. Mark the centre on the edge to be gathered and the flat pattern piece.

3 Match the two pieces and pin in the centre and at the other end. Continue pinning between the inserted pins to distribute the fullness evenly along the length.

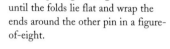

4 Pull up the gathering threads until the folds lie flat and wrap the ends around the other pin in a figure-of-eight.

5 Pin along the folds to hold the gathers in place. The gathers can be basted, or stitch carefully across the pins, using the point of small scissors to straighten the gathers as you sew.

Above: Gathering has been made into a design feature on this velvet top.

Shirring (Gathering elastic)

This is a pretty, stretchy, gathered panel that hugs close to the body. It is used for young children's clothes and to gather sleeves into cuffs. For this technique, shirring elastic rather than thread is wound on to the bobbin in the usual way and fitted into the bobbin case. Set the machine for a long straight stitch and sew several lines of stitches from the right side. Use the side of the foot as a guide for subsequent rows. It may help to hold the fabric taut as you stitch. Work slowly so that the stitch lines are even.

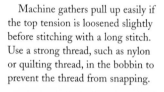

Smocking

Smocking is a decorative technique that has been used all over the world. It is an ornamental way to control fullness in fabric. The smocked panel has a degree of elasticity, making it comfortable to wear. It was traditionally used to make practical smocks for agricultural workers, but nowadays it is more commonly used for baby wear.

There are several ways to gather fabric for smocking. The method you choose depends on the type of fabric to be smocked. Gingham fabric is particularly associated with smocking because the regular squares make it easy to work accurately and evenly. Other fabrics have regular dots or tiny motifs that can also be used as a spacing guide. If the fabric is plain or has an all-over pattern, you can use a smocking transfer sheet. There are different spacings of dots on these sheets to suit a variety of fabrics. The lighter-weight the fabric,

the closer the dots should be. As a guide, light-weight fabrics generally require dots spaced between 5–12mm/ ¼–½in.

Gathering

The gathered section of a piece of fabric often looks completely different from the actual fabric. The way the fabric is gathered can change the surface pattern dramatically and it is advisable to try out different ways of gathering to see what happens.

Gingham fabrics can be stitched at the edge of each square to produce

tucks in alternate colours, or stitched in the middle of the light squares to produce a dark panel or vice versa.

Fabrics with small motifs or dots may look plain when gathered. The dots or motifs can form lines across the tucks to give a striped effect. These lines also help to keep your stitching straight. Match the colour of the motif for a strong design.

Subtle all-over cotton prints look very much the same when gathered. This type of fabric looks good with smocking worked in thread colours that tone in with the fabric.

Getting started

1 Cut a piece of smocking transfer to fit across the width of the fabric. Place the paper dot side down on the wrong side of the fabric and press with a hot iron to transfer the dots.

2 Some fabrics have dots or a regular pattern that you can use as a guide for the gathering stitches. If the dots are too far apart, you can take an extra stitch between each one.

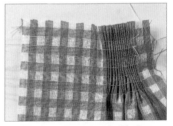

3 Gingham squares make ideal guidelines for smocking. You can take a stitch on the lines between the squares, or stitch into the centre of alternate squares.

FINISHING THE SMOCKING

• Once the smocking is complete pin it, embroidered side down, on the ironing board.

• Hold a steam iron above the tucks and use the steam to set the folds and the stitches.

• Leave to dry. Carefully untie the thread ends, then pull out each of the gathering threads.

Working a smocking sample

Try a small sample of gathering on your chosen fabric to find out the best spacing of the running stitches and to work out the width of fabric required. Generally allow three to four times the width of fabric. A 15–20cm/6–8in piece of fabric, for example, will produce approximately 5cm/2in of smocking. The amount of fabric also depends on the thickness of the fabric and the spacing of the dots. Measure the fabric before and after gathering, and multiply the width to fit the yoke (shoulder) or garment section.

Different stitches give varying amounts of control in smocking. Stem and cable stitch hold the tucks quite firmly and are good outline stitches, usually worked along the top edge, whereas wave stitch produces a much looser effect. Whichever stitches you choose, remember that an even tension is as important in smocking as in knitting. A piece of smocking should "give" quite easily. If you stitch to a tight tension, allow extra width in the fabric to compensate.

Work a small sample first on your chosen fabric before smocking a garment or soft furnishing item to establish the correct tension.

1 Cut the required width of fabric. Mark dots on the wrong side with a transfer sheet if necessary. Cut a long length of strong thread and tie a knot in the end. Work across the fabric with running stitch, picking up a couple of threads at each mark. Complete all rows in the same way.

2 Hold all the gathering threads together and pull up until the folds are close together but still slightly loose. Tie pairs of thread ends together securely. Turn the gathered fabric over so that the tucks are facing upwards. Ease the tucks until they are evenly spaced and straight.

3 Work a row of stem stitch along the top of the tucks. It is easier to follow a guideline to keep the stitching straight. The pattern of this fabric has produced lines of dark blue dots to stitch along. Otherwise open the tucks slightly as you stitch to keep level with a gathering thread.

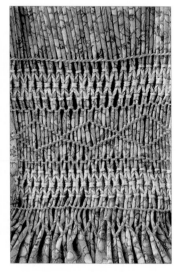

4 Continue stitching bands of smocking stitches across the tucks. Count the tucks and plan the placement of zigzag and diamond patterns carefully. Choose stem or cable stitch for the last row for stability, or a zigzag stitch such as chevron stitch to release the gathers.

Above: A single-colour thread makes a strong contrast on this background.

Above: Subtle all-over cotton prints look most effective when smocked in thread colours that tone in with the fabric.

Smocking stitches

It is the delicate stitching on the surface of smocking which holds the rows of tucked fabric together.

Honeycomb stitch

This stitch can be worked directly on top of the dots or on gathered tucks.

1 Take a small stitch at the top left to secure the thread, then pick up a few threads at the second and then the first dot.

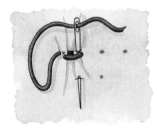

2 Take a second stitch over the first then slide the needle under the fabric to the dot below.

Above: Making a stitch sampler is a good method of learning which stitches you enjoy working, and which threads work well on your chosen fabric. Try working bands of stitches across the fabric and arrange them into a pleasing composition.

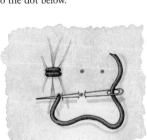

3 Work two stitches to pull the next two dots together.

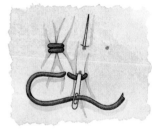

4 Take the needle back up to the dot in the row above.

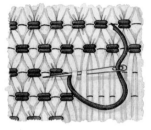

5 Continue working backwards and forwards across the rows in this way.

Cable stitch

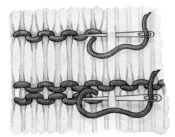

Pick up every tuck in turn, keeping the needle absolutely straight.

Stem stitch/Outline back stitch

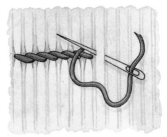

Take back stitches through each tuck, keeping the thread below the needle.

Chevron stitch

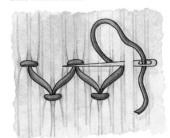

This is similar to surface honeycomb stitch, but the diagonal thread goes across two tucks rather than one.

Wave stitch

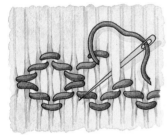

Start in the middle on the left. Take a stitch through two tucks and bring the needle out between them. Stitch over the next two tucks, continuing up in a diagonal. Bring the needle out below the stitches to work back down.

Surface honeycomb stitch

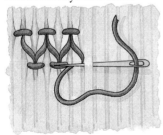

Start at the top left. Stitch through two tucks and bring the needle out between them. Take a stitch below, through the same tuck, then stitch over two tucks, bringing the needle out in the middle as before.

Above: This piece of textural embroidery uses a technique called "gauging" which is similar to smocking but without the smocking stitches. The fabric is gathered with rows of running stitches and supported with a backing fabric.

Hand embroidery stitches

Decorate garments and fashion accessories with these simple embroidery stitches, or use them to embellish soft furnishings such as cushions, table linen or the corner of a pillowcase. Experiment with different weights of thread (floss) and colour combinations on a spare piece of fabric until you get the desired effect. The smaller stitches can be scattered over a large background area or used to create texture on top of other stitches.

Lazy daisy stitch

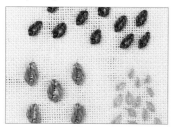

Lazy daisy stitch is a single chain stitch caught down with a small straight stitch at one end. Stitch it in rows or scatter the stitches to create texture. Most threads are suitable, but varying the weight of the thread will alter the size of stitch.

Work the stitch as shown in the diagram, making each loop a similar size. Finish each stitch with a tiny straight stitch to anchor it in place.

French knots

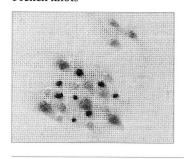

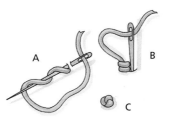

French knots add texture and colour when scattered over fabric and can also be used *en masse* to fill a shape with subtle shading and rich texture.

Bring the needle and thread up through the fabric. Take a small stitch where the thread emerged. Twist the thread around the needle twice (A) then gently pull the needle through (B). Stitch back through the fabric at the side of the knot (C).

Straight stitch

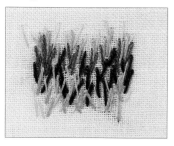

Straight stitch is quick to work and useful for covering large areas with texture. Add shading by stitching in various tones of the same colour, or by using several colours of fine thread in the needle at one time.

Work individual straight stitches over the fabric, varying the size and direction at will. Overlap the stitches to create areas of dense texture.

Back stitch

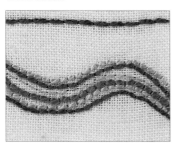

Back stitch is a fine line stitch that can be curved or angular, depending on the length of the stitches. Try using different weights of thread (floss).

Work back stitch from right to left, inserting the needle at the end of the previous stitch. Bring it back out at the start of the next stitch. Keep each stitch the same size and avoid pulling the thread tight or leaving it loose.

Whipped back stitch

Whipped back stitch can be worked in one colour to create a heavy line resembling fine cord, or in contrasting colours for a decorative effect. Try using a different weight of thread for the back stitch and the whip stitch.

Work a row of 5mm/¼in long back stitches. Thread a needle with another colour or weight of thread and slip it under each back stitch without going into the fabric.

Buttonhole stitch and blanket stitch

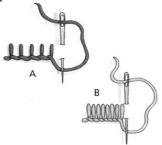

Buttonhole and blanket stitch are essentially the same, except for the way they are spaced. The space between each blanket stitch matches the length of the vertical stitch (A). With buttonhole stitch, the stitches are worked close together (B).

Work both types of stitch from left to right. Space the stitches as required, pulling the needle through over the top of the working thread.

Running stitch

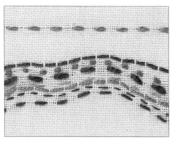

Running stitch can be a tiny prick stitch, a line of basting or a near-solid line, depending on the length of the stitches and the spacing between each. In embroidery, running stitch is worked as a single line or in multiple rows to fill larger areas.

Take the needle in and out across the fabric. Several stitches can be "run" on the needle at one time before it is pulled through the fabric.

Darning and patching

Fabric may need some repair work when an area becomes worn or gives way completely due to constant wear or an accidental tear. Preventive strengthening measures can be taken in certain garments, such as decorative patches on elbows and knees, and rivets on jeans or work-wear pockets. Garments and soft furnishings can also be reinforced before sewing on buttons and pockets.

Darning by hand

Choose a thread for darning that matches the fabric colour as closely as possible. Use one that is slightly thinner than the fabric threads, otherwise the darning will be too thick.

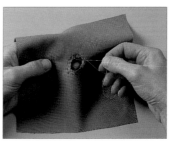 

1 Work with a long length of thread. Begin by basting a circle or square of small running stitches around the outside edge of the worn area.

2 Work small running stitches backwards and forwards across the fabric within the marked area. Leave a slight loop at the end of each row so that the darn doesn't become too tight. At the worn area, leave the thread lying in parallel rows across the hole and work running stitches on each side.

3 Turn the work so that the laid threads are horizontal. Begin to weave over and under the stitches and fabric threads until the entire area is covered with a woven patch. Avoid pulling the threads tight.

Darning by machine

Machine darning is suitable for strengthening worn areas such as the knees of trousers, but can be rather solid if used to fill a hole. Use a darning foot on the machine and stitch with finer thread in a colour to match the fabric. Set the machine for straight stitch and reduce the stitch length to zero.

1 Baste a circle of running stitches around the outside of the worn area. If possible, fit the garment into an embroidery hoop so that the fabric lies flat against the needle plate. Lower the darning foot and work parallel rows of stitching fairly close together backwards and forwards across the marked area.

2 Stop with the needle in the fabric and turn the hoop until the stitches lie across the other way. Stitch more parallel rows slightly further apart to form a stitched grid over the marked area. If filling a hole, turn the hoop back around and work a third set of parallel rows across the hole.

Hand patch
This type of patch is normally used to repair garments. To make the patch less obvious, cut the fabric to match the colour and pattern of the worn area as closely as possible.

1 Cut a patch 3–4cm/1¼–1½in larger than the worn area. Baste it 5mm/¼in from the raw edge and notch any curves. Turn under and baste the raw edge. Work small hemming stitches to secure the patch.

2 On the wrong side, trim away the worn fabric, leaving a 5mm/¼in allowance. Work overcasting or buttonhole stitch over the raw edges without stitching into the front side of the patch.

Machine patch
This quick and easy patch is a hard-wearing way of repairing most utility items around the home. Use fabric from another similar item or pre-wash a new piece of fabric to soften it. Stitch the patch with a matching thread.

1 Cut a square or rectangular patch about 2–3cm/¾–1¼in larger than the worn area and baste it in position on the right side, matching the grain of the fabric. Machine zigzag over the raw edge to secure the patch.

2 Turn the garment over and trim the worn areas of the patch to 9mm/ ⅜in. Machine zigzag over the raw edge. The patch will have two rows of zigzag stitching showing on the right side of the fabric.

Right-angled tear

1 Bring the edges of the tear together by loosely oversewing them. Beginning and ending 5mm/¼in beyond each end of the tear, work tiny stitches across the tear.

2 On a worn garment or pocket tear, iron a square of iron-on interfacing to the wrong side before working the stitches. Pin the pocket back in position and re-stitch over the repair.

3 A button can be replaced over a right-angled tear once this has been repaired with interfacing and machine stitching.

Buttonholes

Unlike buttons, buttonholes are solely functional rather than decorative and normally match the colour of the garment. Take into account the design of the garment and the fabric used before deciding what sort of buttonhole to sew. Hand-worked buttonholes are suitable for soft and delicate fabrics; bound or piped buttonholes give a more tailored look; and machine-sewn buttonholes can be used on more casual garments.

Above: Luxury fabrics need perfect stitching, especially on details such as the buttonholes.

Buttonhole size

Dress patterns include the button size, with the corresponding buttonhole position and length marked, but these need to be checked to see if they match your own choice of buttons and fabric, and altered if necessary.

1 The shape and size of the button will determine the size of the buttonhole. The minimum length required is the diameter of the button plus its thickness and an extra 3mm/⅛in for ease.

2 To measure a shaped or rounded button, wrap a thin strip of paper around the widest part and pin the ends together. Slip the strip off the button and fold in half for the buttonhole length. Add 3mm/⅛in for ease.

BUTTONHOLE POSITION

The position of buttonholes should be marked, along with darts and centre lines, after the pattern pieces are cut out. Buttonholes are not usually worked until quite late in the making process and should be marked once again with basting lines on the right side just before they are stitched.

• Baste along the straight grain of fabric, slightly longer than the proposed buttonhole, and mark the buttonhole length with pins.

• Baste across the first line to show the finished length.

• Horizontal buttonholes are stronger than vertical ones and will close when under any strain.

• Horizontal buttonholes begin 3mm/⅛in to the seam side of the centre line. This allows room for the shank of the button and keeps the centre lines in place.

• On centre front or back openings, vertical buttonholes tend to gape and make the button pop out when put under strain. They are used on loose shirts or where there is a narrow front band. On women's clothing make sure that one of the buttonholes is positioned between the bust points. Space the other buttonholes accordingly.

• Vertical buttonholes begin on the centre line, 3mm/⅛in above the actual button position. This allows for the natural tendency of buttons to pull downwards.

Hand- or machine-stitched buttonholes?

Buttonholes are worked once the garment is complete. Baste the position of the buttonhole through all layers. For hand-sewn buttonholes, use a 45cm/18in length of strong thread or buttonhole twist in the needle. Hand-worked buttonholes have a round end where the button lies and a square end opposite.

Machine-stitched buttonholes are suitable for casual clothes and men's shirts. You will be able to machine stitch buttonholes if your machine has a zigzag stitch, but most automatic machines have an in-built mechanism that alters the width and direction at the touch of a button.

Use a clear-view buttonhole foot on the machine so that you can see your markings on the fabric. This foot has grooves on the underside to guide the fabric so that the slot between the rows of satin stitch is the right width.

By machine

1 Mark the position of the buttonhole along the straight grain with basting thread. Work the first side, finishing with the needle on the right-hand side.

2 Work the bar across the bottom and continue up the second side, finishing with the needle on the outside edge.

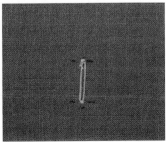

3 Work a bar across the top then use several very small straight stitches to anchor the thread. Trim the thread ends and cut carefully between the rows of satin stitch to open the buttonhole. Use small embroidery scissors or a seam ripper for this.

By hand

1 Cut the buttonhole exactly along a straight thread. Use small embroidery scissors or special adjustable buttonhole scissors. On light-weight fabrics, use a seam ripper.

2 Take the needle through the facing about 2.5cm/1in from the buttonhole and bring it out at the opposite end to where the button will be. Take the needle through the slot and work 3mm/⅛in buttonhole stitches along the first side.

3 Oversew stitches in a fan shape around the button end of the buttonhole. Work buttonhole stitches down the second side, making the stitches the same length as those on the other side.

4 Slip the needle between the two layers of fabric and work several bars of thread across the end of the buttonhole. Work blanket stitch over the bars, keeping the loops facing into the buttonhole. Sew in the thread ends on the wrong side.

Bound buttonholes

Bound buttonholes give a neat tailored appearance and are suitable for light-weight, closely woven fabrics. They are begun before the facing has been attached and are completed at a later stage. It is essential to make and work each buttonhole exactly the same size, so careful, accurate marking is required.

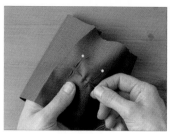

1   Mark the position of the buttonhole with tailor's tacks (through both layers if there is a self-facing) then cut the layers apart.

2   Cut a piece of fabric 5cm/2in wide and 3cm/1¼in longer than the buttonhole. Pin this centrally over the tailor's tacks with right sides together.

3   Mark the buttonhole with basting thread. Beginning on one side, stitch a rectangle 3mm/⅛in away from the thread. Leave the needle in the fabric to turn the corner and carefully count the stitches to work the other side exactly the same distance away.

4   Once the rectangle is complete, trim the thread ends. Cut a slit down the centre of the rectangle and cut carefully into each corner.

5   Pull the fabric rectangle through to the wrong side. Fold the fabric to form an inverted pleat at each end, with the folds of the binding meeting in the centre of the slot. Oversew each end securely.

6   When you are ready to complete the facing, slash along the tailor's tacks and pin the facing over the back of the buttonhole. Turn under the edge and hem an oval shape on the wrong side.

ROULEAUX LOOPS

A rouleau is a self-filled fabric tube used to make single or continuous fabric loops that can be used as a button fastening. Rouleaux loops are sewn into a garment between the main fabric and the facing.

• Cut a bias strip four times the desired finished width. Steam press to remove the excess stretch and fold it in half with right sides together. Stitch down the centre of the folded strip. Slide a rouleau turner into the tube and hook the end. Pull the tube through.

• On the right side of the fabric, baste parallel lines to mark the seam line and the depth of the loops. Plan and mark the loop position and width with thread. Pin the tubing in a curve to the fabric within the guidelines.

• Secure the tubing with diagonal basting and pin the facing in place. Baste along the seam lines and check the loops before stitching the seam.

Piped buttonholes

1 Work these buttonholes before the facing is complete. Mark the position with basting thread. For the piping, cut a 2.5cm/1in wide fabric strip on the straight grain. Iron fusible web to the wrong side, remove the backing and fold the strip lengthways. Press to seal the layers. Trim to 5mm/¹/₄in.

2 Cut two lengths of piping longer than the buttonhole and pin along the marked buttonhole line, with raw edges touching. Baste along the centre of each piece of piping, without catching the facing as well. Work all the buttonholes to the same stage each time for accuracy.

3 Baste the folded edges of the piping together. Trim the piping to 9mm/³/₈in from the end of the buttonhole. Mark the buttonhole ends with tailor's chalk. Beginning in the middle of one piece of piping, stitch to the mark, along to the other end and back to the middle.

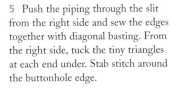

4 Repeat for the second side, counting the stitches to ensure each side is the same length. On the wrong side, cut between the parallel rows of stitching and carefully into each corner.

5 Push the piping through the slit from the right side and sew the edges together with diagonal basting. From the right side, tuck the tiny triangles at each end under. Stab stitch around the buttonhole edge.

Below: Choose a thread to complement the colour scheme when stitching buttonholes.

6 When you are ready to complete the facing, pin the facing over the back of the buttonhole and slash along the buttonhole line. Turn under the edge and hem stitch an oval shape on the wrong side.

Buttons

Buttons are more than just functional fasteners; they can also be a decorative feature. Changing the buttons can alter the look of a garment. When cheap buttons are replaced with better quality ones, a garment can look more expensive than it actually is.

Buttons come in an amazing range of styles, colours, shapes and sizes, and need to be chosen carefully to suit the garment. Pin buttons in place to find which are most suitable before making any buttonholes. Buttons are sewn on the buttonhole line 3mm/ ⅛in from the end of the buttonhole.

Carefully pin the garment closed, matching the centre front line, and insert a pin through the buttonhole to mark the button's position. Use a strong thread to match the colour of the button. The length of thread shank between the underside of the button and the fabric should equal the thickness of the garment at the buttonhole, plus a little room for ease of movement.

Two-hole button

1 Make two tiny back stitches where you are going to sew the button. Thread the needle through one of the holes on the button and hold the button in position. With the holes either horizontal or vertical to match the direction of the buttonhole, make the first stitch. Insert a pin under the thread and sew on the button.

2 Remove the pin and bring the needle out underneath the button. Wrap the thread around several times between the button and the garment to create a shank, then take the needle through to the wrong side.

3 On the wrong side work blanket stitch over the thread bars. This step is often omitted but does reinforce the thread and helps prevent buttons from falling off at a later date.

Four-hole button

This is sewn on in the same way as a two-hole button. Either sew through the holes to form two bars or work a cross stitch. Work the shank and blanket stitch bars as for a two-hole button.

Shank button

A shank button has a plastic or metal loop or stem on the wrong side for fixing. Attach the button with tiny stitches worked through the hole in the shank. If the fabric is very bulky, a thread shank will be required as well. Align the narrowest part of the shank with the buttonhole.

Covered buttons

Buttons can be covered to match the fabric for a more subtle effect or when you can't find suitable buttons. Covered buttons also look very effective in a contrasting fabric to match piping or binding. Self-cover buttons can be decorated with a number of embroidery techniques to create unique designs. Personalize your buttons with tiny cross-stitch initials or appliqué a different design on each button.

Self-cover buttons are either plastic or metal. They are covered with a circle of fabric that is stitched or fitted, using a small tool that you can buy. Use plastic buttons if the garment is likely to be washed regularly and metal buttons if it is to be dry-cleaned, making sure that the button type suits the fabric.

Covering buttons by hand

1 Cut a circle of fabric as indicated in the manufacturer's instructions. If the fabric frays, iron light-weight interfacing to the wrong side before cutting out. Work tiny running stitches around the edge of the circle.

2 Hold the button top in the middle of the fabric circle and pull the thread up tightly. Ease the gathers into position and sew the end in securely. Fit the back over the shank and press until it clicks into place.

Using a plastic tool

1 Cut a circle of fabric. Select the corresponding hole in the plastic tool and centre the fabric on top. Push the button top into the recess so that the fabric edges turn over. Fit the back over the shank and press into place.

Centring a motif

1 Cut the required circle from tracing paper and hold it over the fabric to find the best area to cover the button. Pin and cut out, carefully centring any motif. Cover the button. The plastic tool has a hole in the base for you to check the position before fitting the button back.

Right: Buttons are made from many different materials such as plastic, metal, wood and leather, or can be covered in fabric.

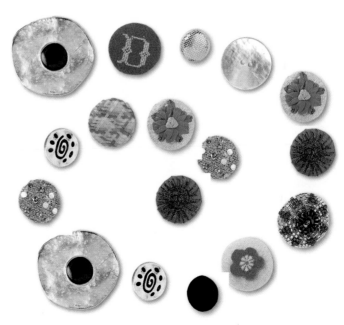

Fasteners for fabrics

Fasteners come in a variety of types and sizes to suit different fabrics. They are worked through two layers of fabric, or single fabric and interfacing. Hooks and eyes are sewn on the wrong side and are invisible when in use. Add fastenings once the garment is complete. If the fabric edges touch use a hook and eye, but if they overlap use a hook and bar. The hook is sewn in the same position in both cases.

Hooks and eyes

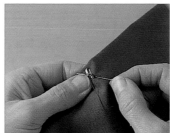
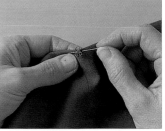

1 Hold the hook 3–5mm/¹/₈–¹/₄in back from the folded edge on the wrong side. Work several stitches over the hook end to hold it in place, making sure it does not show on the right side.

2 Bring the needle through the layers of fabric and out next to one of the loops on the hook. Work buttonhole stitch around both loops to secure the hook to the fabric. Fasten the eye into the hook.

3 Position the eye on the other side of the garment so that it extends over the edge by 3–5mm/¹/₈–¹/₄in. Take a back stitch across the eye to hold it in place and unfasten. Work buttonhole stitch around the two loops to secure.

Buttonhole bars (Thread eyes)

Eyelets

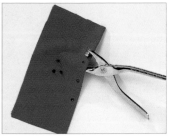

1 Use thread loops to secure single buttons at the neck edge where they are worked on the fold of fabric. Using strong thread or buttonhole twist, work several large stitches of the required length through the fabric. Allow extra length for ease, depending on the button thickness.

2 Work buttonhole stitches over the thread loop, keeping the stitches straight and close together. Make sure that the loop doesn't twist as you cover it with stitches. Finish off with a couple of tiny back stitches on the wrong side.

1 Mark the position of the eyelets with a pencil then punch a hole through the fabric at each mark. The hole should be just large enough for the eyelet to fit through.

2 Insert the eyelet from the right side of the fabric and use eyelet pliers to fit it into the hole.

Press studs (Snap fasteners)

These are quick-opening fasteners useful for cushion covers and on overlapping garment edges where there is little strain. They come in black, silver or plastic, and in a range of sizes to suit different fabrics. Sew the thinner knob of the stud on the underside of the top layer of the opening. Use a strong thread, as finer threads tend to fray against the sharp metal edge of the holes. The stitches should be worked through the facing and interfacing only.

1 Work a few small back stitches where the base of the stud is to go. Hold the stud in position and work four or five buttonhole stitches into each hole to secure it in place.

2 Feed a pin through the fabric and up through the stitched stud. Fit the other half of the stud on top and position the other side of the garment on top. Hold the stud in place and sew on with buttonhole stitches.

Poppers (Rivets)

There are many different types of popper (rivet) fasteners on the market suitable for a wide range of casual clothes. The sets of poppers come with a small tool that you use with a hammer to fix them in position. Always follow the manufacturer's instructions.

It is advisable to try out the technique on a spare piece of fabric first. Always double-check the position of the poppers as they can't be removed once they have been hammered into place.

1 Mark the position of the poppers (rivets) on the top layer of the garment and use a pin to transfer the position to the lower layer. Fit the appropriate sections into the tool and place on each side of the fabric.

Velcro

This is an easy-to-use fastener that can be substituted for most other types of fastening. It is useful for children's wear and where adjustments are required, such as in maternity wear and for those who have difficulty with other fasteners.

Velcro is available in strips and in small circles. One side has plastic hooks which attach to the soft loops on the other side. Self-adhesive Velcro is used on soft furnishings.

1 Select the hook piece of Velcro and attach it to the top fabric with small hem stitches.

2 Tap the hammer sharply against the tool to join the sections.

3 Fit the sections for the lower part of the popper into the plastic tool and secure them into the fabric, using the hammer. Make sure the lower sections align with the top part.

2 Check the position of the lower layer and sew on the loop pieces of Velcro by hand or machine.

Choosing and inserting zippers

Zippers are one of the most common methods of fastening items and there is one to suit every fabric and sewing requirement. They fall into three categories – those with metal or plastic teeth (chain zippers), those with interlocking nylon or polyester coils (coil zippers) and invisible zippers.

Invisible zippers look like a seam on the right side of the fabric. Chain zippers are stronger but fairly bulky, and coiled zippers are more flexible but can pull apart under any strain. Choose a zipper to suit the fabric weight and type of garment: for example, a jacket requires an open-ended zipper, whereas jeans and trousers need heavy-duty zippers.

Skirt or neckline zipper
These are the most common weight of zipper and are available in different lengths. This zipper is designed to be

inserted in the seam of a garment, down the centre back or on one side.

Light-weight zipper
The tape on a light-weight zipper is much finer than that on ordinary zippers. This makes it more delicate, but also more flexible than ordinary zippers and it is ideal for fine fabrics. It is available in lengths from 18–56cm/7–22in.

Jeans (brass) zipper
This is a heavy-weight zipper made with large brass teeth on a very strong

tape. It is quite bulky and only suitable for trousers made in heavy-weight fabrics such as denim or corduroy.

Open-ended zipper
There are several weights of open-ended zippers to suit different applications. Jacket zippers are available to match the heavy brass jeans zipper and there are lighter-weight chunky zippers for other garments. Dress-weight zippers are also available in an open-ended version. These are available in different lengths.

Hand-sewing a zipper

This method is used to insert zippers into sheer or delicate fabrics. It is fairly strong but shouldn't be used where there will be a lot of strain.

1 Stitch the seam to the bottom of the zipper opening. Hand or machine baste the zipper opening and press open. Position the zipper along the seam line and pin in place.

2 From the right side, baste 5mm/¼in to each side of the seam line. Prick stitch along the basting lines, making the tiny stitches about 3–5mm/⅛–¼in apart.

3 Pull the basting thread out from the seam line of the zipper opening.

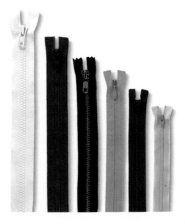

Above from left to right: jacket zipper, open-ended zipper, jeans (brass) zipper, invisible zipper, skirt-weight zipper and light-weight zipper.

Inserting a semi-concealed zipper

This method is used for centre front or back positions in a garment, or a slot in a side or back seam of soft furnishings.

1 Machine stitch the seam up to the bottom of the zipper opening. Turn under the seam allowance and baste down 5mm/¹⁄₄in away from the fold.

2 Place the pull tab of the zipper 5mm/¹⁄₄in below the top seam line. Pin the fabric on each side of the zipper so that the folds run up the centre of the teeth.

3 Diagonal baste the folds together to prevent them opening while stitching. Baste along the guidelines and remove the pins. Using a zipper foot attachment, stitch just outside the basting lines down one side.

4 Leave the needle in the fabric then turn to stitch across the bottom and back up the other side.

Top: Zippers are a good choice for small children's outfits.

Inserting a concealed zipper

This is often used to insert a zipper into the side seam of a skirt. It is ideal for cushions and other items of soft furnishings and makes an unobtrusive and neat fastening, since a fold of fabric overlaps the zipper so that it cannot be seen. This doesn't affect the fit because the stitching line is brought forward 3mm/¹⁄₈in on the back section and set back 3mm/¹⁄₈in on the front section.

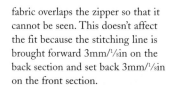

1 Machine stitch the seam up to the bottom of the zipper opening. Press the opening along the seam line on the back section of the garment. Fold the seam allowance 3mm/¹⁄₈in out from the pressed line and baste.

2 Baste a guideline on the front side 7.5mm/³⁄₈in from the fold. Position the pull tab 5mm/¹⁄₄in below the top seam line. Pin and baste the back section next to the zipper teeth. Machine stitch close to the fold.

3 Pin and baste the front section in place, matching the original seam lines. Machine stitch along the guideline. Leave the needle in the fabric then turn and stitch across the bottom of the zipper.

Making tassels

Tassels are extremely versatile. They come in all shapes and sizes, and are used to decorate garments and cushions or to make very effective tie-backs. Although a tremendous choice is available, sometimes it is not possible to get exactly the right colour or type of thread, but simple tassels are easy to make. Embroidery threads, crochet cottons and tapestry or crewel wools (yarns) are all suitable, depending on the effect you want.

Simple tassel

1 Cut a piece of card (card stock) slightly wider than the finished tassel length. Wrap thread around the card until you have wound on enough to make the required size of tassel.

2 Slip a double length of cord under the threads. Tie the double cord to hold the threads together. Hold the threads securely in your hand then snip along the bottom edge.

3 Fold a single thread into a long loop and hold it against the tassel, with the loop at the top. Wrap the other end several times around the tassel to create a "neck".

4 Slip the working end through the loop and pull the other end to take the loop under the wrapping. Snip the thread ends and trim the tassel neatly.

Right: Tassels are quick and fun to make. Use toning shades of one colour for a subtle effect.

Corded tassel

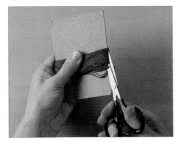

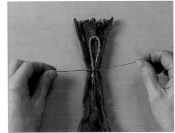

1 Cut a piece of card (card stock) slightly wider than the finished tassel length. Wrap thread around the card until you have enough to make the required size of tassel. Cut along one edge.

2 Tie a large knot in a piece of cord to form a loop and place it on top of the bundle of threads so that the knot lies just below the mid-point. Tie a strong thread around the tassel above the knot.

Above and below: These elaborate tassels are ideal for soft furnishing items such as tie-backs or to decorate the corners of throws.

3 Ease the threads evenly around the knot to cover it, then let the top threads drop down over the knot to form the tassel.

4 Wrap thread around the tassel to make a "neck" (see Simple tassel, steps 3 and 4). Carefully trim the ends of the threads level.

Making cushions

Cushions add the finishing touch to a room and make it more comfortable and inviting. They can be simple and stylish to complement a classic chair or more adventurous and colourful to jazz up a plain sofa. Use fabric that complements the other fabrics in the room.

Cushions can be filled with a variety of materials. The most luxurious is feather and down, but there are cheaper alternatives such as foam chips and polyester wadding (batting). If you decide to make your own cushion pad, use a heavy-weight calico for the pad cover to prevent the filling from escaping, and pack the cushion pad quite firmly as the contents will settle and flatten once it is in use. Make the cover slightly smaller than the cushion pad

dimensions to ensure the cushion is really plump when made up. By the time you have deducted the seam allowances from a 45cm/18in cover, it will fit snugly over a 45cm/18in cushion pad. If the fabric has a bold design such as stripes, it is a good idea to make a paper pattern to ensure that the designs match where necessary.

You can fit a zipper in any position on the wrong side of a cushion but the simplest place to insert it is 5–7.5cm/2–3in from the top edge.

Zipper fastening

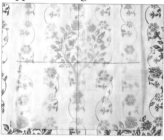

1 Cut the shape of the cushion from tracing paper and mark the centre lines with a felt pen. Position the pattern on the fabric and pin in place. Add seam allowances and cut out.

2 Cut a back panel, adding an extra 4cm/1½in seam allowance. Cut across the panel 7.5–10cm/3–4in from the top edge. Turn under 15mm/⅝in along the top edge of the larger piece and pin to the zipper tape. Baste and machine stitch close to the zipper, using a zipper foot in the machine.

3 Turn under 2cm/¾in along the bottom edge of the narrow piece and baste a guideline 15mm/⅝in from the fold. Pin the folded edge over the zipper so that it just covers the machine stitching.

Above: The motif on this fabric is the ideal size for a cushion.

4 Baste and machine stitch along the basted guideline, using the zipper foot. Remove all basting and open the zipper slightly before sewing the back and front panels together with right sides facing.

Envelope (Overlap) opening

1 An envelope (overlap) opening is a discreet and easy-to-make cushion opening. Cut the front panel the required size plus seam allowances. Cut two pieces for the back, each measuring half the depth of the front plus an extra 7.5cm/3in. Press under a small hem along one long edge of both pieces. Machine stitch in place.

2 On a flat surface, place the front panel right side up. Pin one back panel to the left-hand side and one to the right-hand side, matching raw edges. Overlap the two pieces so that the lower flap comes from the top of the cushion. Pin the side seams. If you prefer not to stitch over pins, baste around the edge.

3 Machine stitch around the edge of the cushion. Keep the stitching at the corners square by leaving the needle in the fabric before swinging the cushion around to stitch the next side. Reverse stitch over the overlap for extra strength. Trim across the corners to reduce bulk and turn through.

Making a flange

Cut a front cushion panel and make a back panel with either an envelope or zipper opening. Baste with wrong sides together. When cutting the flange, if the fabric has an obvious pattern or weave, cut four pieces horizontally and four vertically.

Above: A flange makes a cushion appear much larger. It can be decorated with cord, ribbons or buttons.

1 Cut eight strips of fabric, each 7.5cm/3in wide and 15cm/6in longer than each cushion edge. Fold back one corner of each strip until the raw edges align. Trim diagonally.

2 Pin the corners right sides together and stitch, stopping 15mm/⅝in away from the inside edge. Make two square flange panels in this way and press the corner seams flat.

3 Pin the two flange panels right sides together. Machine stitch around the outside edge. Clip the corners and trim the seams to reduce bulk.

4 Turn the cover right side out. Ease out the corners and press flat. Tuck the basted cushion panels inside the flange then pin and machine stitch.

Flap opening

A flap opening is usually positioned on the front of the cushion. The flap can be shaped in various ways and fastened using buttons, ties, poppers or Velcro. These instructions are for a 45cm/18in cushion. It is a good idea to cut stripes for the front and back panels in the opposite direction to avoid matching problems.

Above: Stripes in opposite directions avoid the problem of difficult matching at seams.

1   Cut a 45 x 60cm/18 x 24in back panel and a 30 x 45cm/12 x 18in flap panel. With right sides together, pin the flap to the top of the back panel. Cut a 45cm/18in square front panel with the top edge on a selvage, or add an allowance for a small hem.

2   Machine stitch 15cm/6in down the sides and along the top edge. Trim the seams and clip the corner. Clip into the seam allowance where the stitching ends on both sides.

3   Turn the flap through, ease out the corners and press. Pin the front panel to the back with right sides together. Stitch around the remaining sides, trim the seam allowances as before, and turn through. Add the fastening of your choice.

Adding cord

Cushions can be decorated by sewing cord around the edges. This is done once the cushion has been made up.

Above: Choose a cord that has the same colour as the fabric or go for a complete contrast to add accent colours.

1   Unpick about 2.5cm/1in of the stitching along the bottom seam. Beginning at this point, hand sew the cord invisibly but securely to the seam line on the front of the cushion.

2   Trim the ends to 2.5cm/1in and tuck them into the gap. Stitch the gap closed, securing the cord ends.

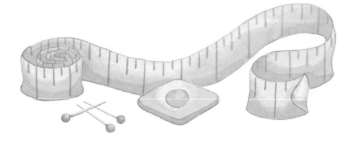

Adding a flanged cord or piping

Both these types of decorative edging have a projecting edge that can be stitched to the cushion panel: on flanged cord it is made from tape, on piping it is a raw fabric edge.

1 Pin the piping along the seam line of the cushion front panel, with the tape or raw edge facing outwards. Clip into the tape to help the cord go around the corners. Machine stitch the cord or piping in place, using a zipper foot in the machine.

2 Pin the back panel on top and baste securely. Machine stitch as close as possible to the cord or piping. Trim across the corners and turn the cushion pad through.

Making a bolster cushion

Bolster cushions are quite different in shape from other cushions. Tubular cushion forms are available in different shapes and sizes.

The cover consists of a tube of fabric with two end panels. These can be flat circles or gathered panels. The opening for the cushion pad is usually along the tube seam. Either leave a gap for hand sewing or insert a zipper.

The end of the bolster cushion can be decorated with a flanged cord or fabric-covered piping cord, or left plain. Finish the end with a matching tassel or a fabric-covered button to complement your colour scheme.

Right: Bolster cushions, once associated with formal furnishings and rigid fillings, can be made to suit almost any style of decor.

1 Measure the length and circumference of the bolster cushion pad and cut a panel that size. Measure the radius of the cushion pad and add a 2.5cm/1in seam allowance. Cut two strips that width to fit across the end of the tube panel. Pin the flanged cord across the short ends of the large panel on the right side. Machine stitch close to the cord, using a zipper foot.

2 With right sides together, pin the end panels on top and machine stitch as close as possible to the cord, using the zipper foot. Work two rows of machine gathering stitches along the outside edge of each end panel.

3 With right sides together, pin and stitch the long seam of the cushion panel. If the cord is very bulky, you will have to hand sew that part of the seam. Gather the tube ends. Insert a tassel cord from the right side and wrap the gathered end as tightly as possible with a piece of strong thread.

Curtain equipment

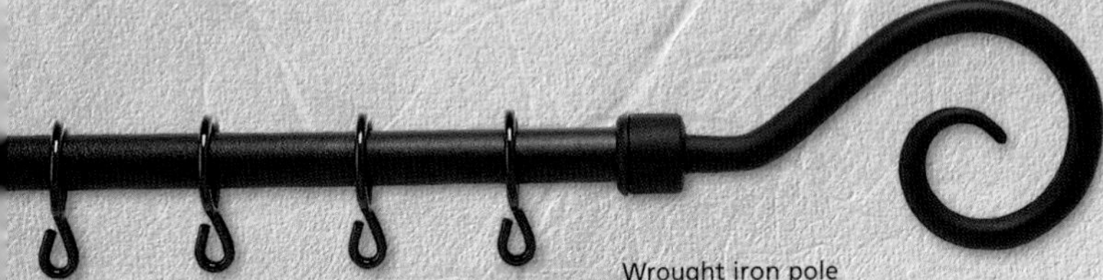

Wrought iron pole

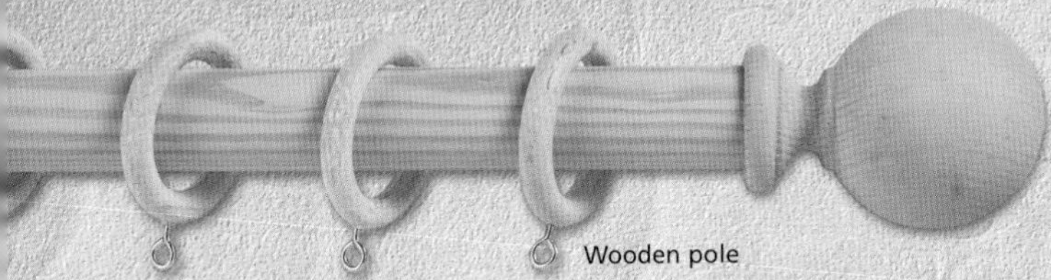

Wooden pole

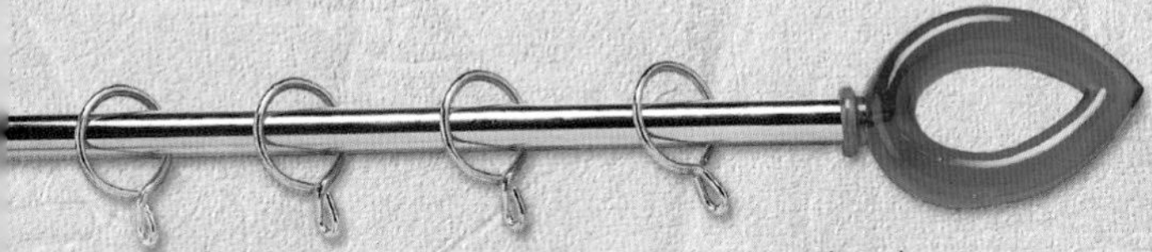

Contemporary curtain pole

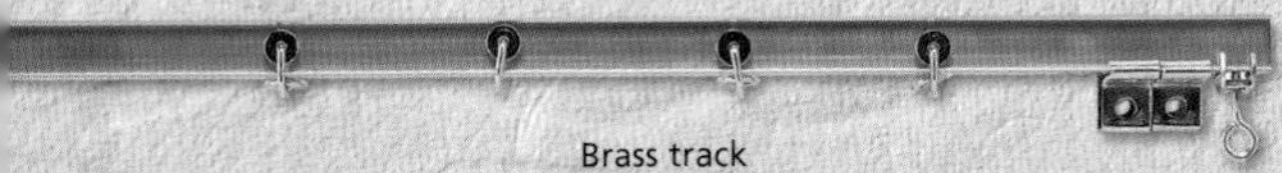

Brass track

Net track

Brass café rod

Hold-back    Hook for a tie-back 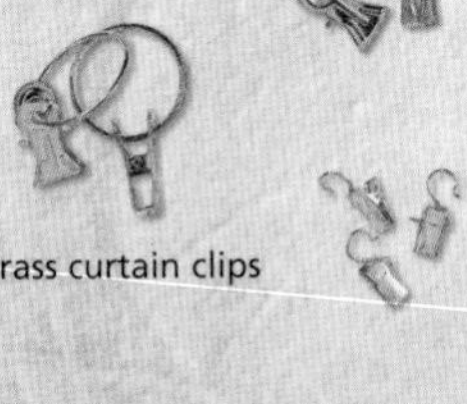   Brass curtain clips

Brass track

This high-quality traditional rail is ideal for conservatories because it can withstand high temperatures without distorting. It has a certain unique design appeal in ultra-modern houses and the metal rollers run very smoothly.

Brass café rod

This beautiful brass rod is too elegant to cover. It can be used with a self-heading curtain, but looks particularly elegant when the curtain is hung from café rod clips.

Contemporary curtain pole

The finials on this retro-look curtain pole are available in a range of shapes and colours to suit your decor. You can choose from three different poles and fit matching tie-backs to create a distinctive and individual look.

Wrought iron pole

Wrought iron poles make a distinct design statement in the home. These poles are less heavy than traditional wrought iron and are suitable for light- to medium-weight fabrics. Several different finials are available.

Wooden pole

Wooden poles are normally supplied with matching curtain rings. They are available in a variety of different wood and paint finishes, and with a choice of carved finials.

Brass curtain clips

Curtain clips are an alternative to traditional hooks. They do away with curtain tapes and are ideal for simple curtains. Curtain clips are spaced evenly along the top of the curtain (in the same way as bulldog clips grip paper), and the hoop at the top of the grip slides on to the pole.

Hold-backs

Hold-backs are used to hold curtains away from the window. With some, the curtain is simply draped over the pole and held in place by the decorative disc, with others a tie-back is used.

Net wire

This steel wire with a plastic coating can be cut to length and simply fitted using hooks and eyes. It is suitable for sheer or light-weight fabrics with a simple self-heading.

Net track

This light-weight, extendible track is suitable for sheer and light-weight fabrics. Some types can be fitted to the window with hooks or fittings. Others have adhesive pads for use with plastic frame windows.

Valance track

A standard valance track is fitted behind the curtain rail fittings and can be bent to fit a bay window. It is strong enough to be used for all weights of valance.

Cord track

Cord tracks are pre-corded to allow easy access for opening and closing curtains without touching them. This type is suitable for straight runs with medium-weight curtains.

PVC curtain track

This basic general-purpose curtain track is easy to fit and to remove for decorating. It is suitable for medium-weight curtains and can be bent into shape.

Curtain hooks

Curtain hooks are made to fit particular curtain tracks. End hooks have a screw to keep them in position. The smaller hooks are used for attaching linings to curtain tape.

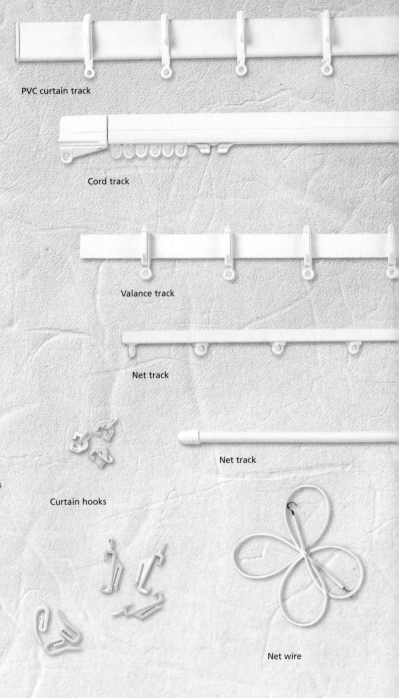

PVC curtain track

Cord track

Valance track

Net track

Net track

Curtain hooks

Net wire

Making curtains

It is not difficult to make professional-looking curtains. All you need is a sewing machine and the ability to sew straight. Curtains cover a window and add a decorative touch to a room, but they also cut out light, provide privacy, reduce noise and add warmth. The type of curtain you choose depends on the shape and position of your window, the depth of the window recess and the effect you want to create.

Sheer curtains on net wires are usually fitted inside the window recess, while tracks or rods are fitted above the window and extend out on each side. How far they extend will depend on the position of the window and the thickness of the fabric. You should be able to pull the curtains almost clear of the window to allow as much light in as possible.

Before you determine the amount of fabric required, you must first decide on the type of rod or track and where it will be fitted. Most curtains are two to three times as wide as the curtain rod or pole, depending on the type of heading. Valances are generally fuller and require about four times the width.

In practice, the width of the fabric will determine the final fullness of the curtains because the number of "drops", or lengths, of fabric sewn together to make the curtain are generally worked out in full or half-widths. Most curtain fabrics are 120cm/48in wide and measurements are rounded up or down to the nearest 60cm/24in. So, for example, on a 200cm/80in wide window each curtain should be anything from 400–600cm/160–240in wide. Two drops on each side would be 480cm/196in, slightly more than twice the width; whereas two and a half drops on each side would be exactly three times the width. Half-widths are stitched to the outside of each curtain.

Joining curtain drops

Curtains must match across each seam and between the two curtains, so extra fabric may have to be bought if a fabric has a large design. Join the fabric selvage to selvage, keeping any half-widths on the outside.

Inside the recess

Curtains that hang inside the recess are normally fitted near the top unless they are café-style curtains. Measure inside the recess in both directions to get the width and the length. Multiply the width by both one-and-a-half and two-and-a-half, then work out the number of drops of fabric required so that it lies between the two measurements. Add about 20cm/8in to the length of each drop for hems.

Outside the recess

Curtain poles and tracks are fitted just above the recess, with the curtain hanging just below the window sill or to reach to the floor. This measurement will be the length of the drop. The width of the curtain depends on the length of the curtain pole or track rather than the width of the recess. Depending on the type of heading tape used (fancy tapes such as pinch pleats or goblets use more fabric), multiply the width by both two and three, then work out the number of drops of fabric required so that it lies between the measurements. Round up rather than down for these curtains. Add about 20cm/8in to the length of each drop for hems.

Above: Plain cream or white fabric always looks elegant at a window. The matching pelmet adds a formal touch.

Above: Unusual black-and-white striped curtains are finished off with a swag and a decorative rose.

Unlined curtains

Unlined curtains are simple to make but can fade in the sunlight. If you are using satin or velvet, sew the hems by hand.

Cut the fabric according to the style of curtain you are making and join the drops as required.

1 Turn under a 12mm/½in hem down each edge and machine stitch.

2 ◄ Turn under 12mm/½in along the bottom edge and then turn up a 5–7.5cm/2–3in hem. Machine stitch, then slip stitch the gaps at each side of the hem.

Lined curtains

Lined curtains hang better than unlined curtains and provide more insulation. Lining is sold in narrower widths than curtain fabric so the same number of drops may require an adjustment of width.

1 Cut the fabric according to the curtain style and join the drops. Cut the lining 15cm/6in shorter and about 13cm/5in narrower than the curtain. Turn up 7.5cm/3in at the bottom of the curtain and a 5cm/2in hem at the bottom of the lining, and stitch.

2 With right sides together, pin the lining so that its hem overlaps the top of the curtain hem by about 2.5cm/1in. Machine stitch the side seams and press the seams open.

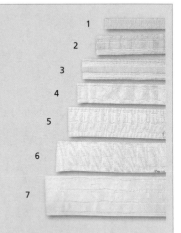

3 Turn the curtain through and centre the lining. Pin along the top edge and baste down each side, making sure the curtain and lining are lying flat. Slip stitch the corners of the hem.

TYPES OF HEADING TAPE

The type of heading tape you choose will determine the look of the curtains and the amount of fabric you need to buy.

• **Narrow tape** – for simple curtains that are fitted inside a recess or underneath a valance.

• **Pencil pleat** – a basic heading tape for curtains that require about twice the width of fabric to look good. The folds are about 12mm/½in wide.

• **Pinch pleat** – one of several fancy headings that need a specific width of fabric to hang properly. They normally require about three times the width and are used in more formal settings.

• **Loose lining tape** – a narrow tape that fits along the top edge of the lining. It fits with standard hooks to the curtain tape.

• **Sheer curtain tape** – a lightweight transparent pencil tape specially made for sheer fabrics. This tape is used if the curtains are to open.

• **Velcro curtain tape** – a pencil tape with bands on the reverse side that stick to Velcro. It is used to fit curtains into window recesses and on to valance boards.

Above: 1 lining tape; 2 sheer Velcro tape; 3 sheer curtain tape; 4 narrow tape; 5 pencil pleat; 6 pencil pleat for Velcro; 7 pinch pleat.

Narrow tape

1 You will need between one-and-a-half times and twice the width for this heading tape. Tie the cords at one end of the curtain tape together.

2 Turn down a 3–5cm/1¼–2in single hem at the top of the curtain. Pin the curtain tape over the raw edge and baste in place. Trim the ends of the tape and turn under.

3 Machine stitch along each edge of the curtain tape. Draw up the cords to the correct width and tie off the other end.

Pencil pleats

Pinch pleats

1 You will need between two and three times the width for this heading tape. Turn down a 2cm/¾in hem along the top edge of the curtain. Draw out the cord at one end of the tape and knot together.

2 Pin the heading tape along the top edge of the curtain, turning the ends underneath the hem. Stitch along the guidelines at the top and bottom edges of the tape.

You will need about three times the width for this heading tape.

1 Attach the tape to the curtains in the same way as pencil pleats, making sure that the tape is facing in the right direction, so that when you pull the tape up the pleats will fan out at the top.

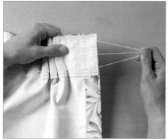

TIP

On very wide curtains, tie the cord ends to a door handle before pulling them up.

3 Pull the cords out singly at first then hold the ends together and ease the curtain to the correct width. Tie the cords to secure and tuck the ends inside between the tape and the curtain.

Detachable lining

This type of lining can be fitted to most curtain tapes and is a good choice where the curtain will be frequently washed or dry cleaned. The lining does not have to be as full as the curtain. Cut the lining so that it is between one-and-a-half times and twice the width of the window or track, and the same length as the curtain. Turn under and sew a double hem down each side of the fabric.

Open the loose lining tape and fit it over the top raw edge of the lining. Pin and machine stitch the tape in place. Trim the end of the tape and turn it under. Pull out the cord and ease the lining to fit the width of the curtain. Turn up a double hem along the bottom edge so that the lining is about 2.5–5cm/1–2in shorter than the curtain and machine stitch. Attach the lining to the curtain tape with standard curtain hooks.

Self-heading

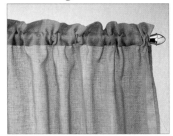

Sheer or net curtains that will stay closed can be hung from spring wires on a narrow window, and from a narrow brass rod or slim pole on a wider window. In each case, the top of the curtain is turned over to form a casing. It is not necessary to join the seams if there are several drops as the selvages are less visible than a seam.

1 Turn up the hem and make the curtain up as for an unlined curtain. Turn down a 3–5cm/1¼–2in hem along the top edge, depending on the width of the spring wire or rod. Machine stitch the hem along the bottom edge then stitch again, 1–2cm/½–¾in away, to make a casing for a rod.

2 Sew in the thread ends and press the curtain. Remove the finial from one end of the curtain rod. Feed the curtain on to the rod or spring wire. Even out the gathers along the length of the curtain. Hang the rod from hooks fitted at each end.

Fitting curtain hooks

Curtain hooks are normally fitted in the middle row of loops on the curtain tape, unless the curtain has to fit on a rail very near the ceiling. Insert a hook every 10–15cm/4–6in along the tape, depending on the weight of fabric. A heavier fabric will need smaller gaps between the hooks. Fit a hook with a screw in the last

space at the left or right, depending on which way the curtain will open. Measure the curtain rail and gather each hooked curtain up to fit on half the rail. The hooks can slide on to the rail or will "snap on" if pushed gently. Close the curtains and re-arrange the pleats so that they spread evenly along the track.

Tied curtain

These are made from a basic unlined curtain which has been machine stitched with a 2cm/³⁄₄in hem along the top edge. These curtains create an informal look.

Ties can be made from cord, ribbon or tape and fitted in the same way as the fabric tapes shown here.

1 Decide on the length of tie required by pinning the centre of a strip of fabric to the curtain and tying the raw edges in a bow over the pole. Work out how many strips are required, spacing them every 10–15cm/4–6in. When calculating the quantity of fabric, remember to add seam allowances.

2 Cut each strip twice the finished width plus a 12mm/¹⁄₂in seam allowance. Fold the strips in half lengthways. Leaving a gap in the middle for turning, machine stitch along the length and across both ends 5mm/¹⁄₄in from the raw edge. Make the ends taper to a point.

3 Trim across the corners and turn through. Ease out the points of the tie with a blunt, narrow tool such as a bodkin or darning needle. Roll the tie so that the seam lies exactly on the edge and press flat. Neatly slip stitch the gap closed.

4 Fold the tie in half crossways and pin the fold on the wrong side of the hem at the top of the curtain. Using good-quality thread, stitch in a square to secure the tie. Sew in the ends of the threads. Stitch the other ties in place evenly across the width of the curtain, in the same way.

Eyelet curtain

1 Make an unlined curtain and turn down and sew a 2.5cm/1in hem along the top edge. Make a mark at 7.5–10cm/3–4in intervals along the top hem of the curtain and an equal distance from the fold. Use the special tool supplied with the eyelets and a hammer to cut a hole in the centre of the hem at each mark.

2 Turn the curtain with the wrong side facing up. Fit the tube section of the eyelet through the hole and drop the ring on top. Cover with the tool and hammer into position.

3 Thread the cord through each hole, leaving a loop to fit over the pole. Tie the ends of the cord in a knot and trim neatly. This type of curtain also looks good on a simple wooden curtain pole.

Café curtain

This is an attractive way to screen the lower half of a window and at the same time allow light through the top half. The curtain normally hangs inside the recess across the window but can be hung across the window from a curtain pole. The width of the curtain will depend on whether it is to hang flat or have soft gathers. Scalloped-top curtains can be made in a single colour or in two contrasting fabrics, as shown here.

Draw a paper pattern for the curtain top. Decide on the length, making sure the finished curtain will reach the window sill, and add a 5cm/2in hem allowance. The end of the tabs can be any shape – simply alter the pattern below before cutting out. Try out your paper pattern over the rod first before cutting the fabric.

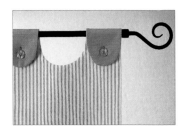

1 Fold the pattern over to make a straight edge as shown and pin to the fabric. Draw around the pattern with tailor's chalk and move along to complete the scallops. Cut out. If desired, cut contrasting fabric to match.

2 With right sides together, sew down the sides and around the curves. Trim the seams to 5mm/¹⁄₄in. Notch the outward curves as shown and clip the inward curves. Turn the curtain through and press.

3 Work a vertical buttonhole if required on each tab. Fold the tab over the pole and check the buttonhole position. (The button will sit at the top of the buttonhole). Sew the buttons in place. Fit the curtain over the pole and pin up the hem. Make the hem 1–2.5cm/¹⁄₂–1in shorter on the inside of the curtain.

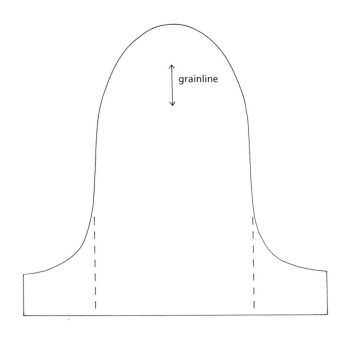

grainline

Above: A café-style curtain is a good choice where both privacy and good natural light are required.

Left: Enlarge this template to the desired size, and so that it repeats evenly across the width of your fabric.

INDEX

SUPPLIERS

United Kingdom

Barnyarns Ltd
PO Box 28
Thirsk
North Yorkshire, YO7 3YN
for sewing and embroidery supplies

Bogod Machine Company
50–52 Great Sutton Street
London, EC1V ODJ
for sewing machines and overlockers

Coats Crafts
McMullen Road
Darlington
Co. Durham, DL1 1YQ
*for machine embroidery and
sewing threads*

Delicate Stitches
339 Kentish Town Road
Kentish Town
London
NW5 2TJ
for fine natural fabrics

DMC Creative World
Pullman Road
Wigston
Leicestershire, LE18 2DY
*for counted-thread fabrics, embroi-
dery thread and crewel wool*

Duttons for Buttons
3 Church Street
Ilkley, LS29 9DR
branches in Harrogate, Keighley,
York and Leeds
for buttons

Harrison Drape
Bradford Street
Birmingham, B12 0PE
for curtain equipment

House of Smocking
1 Ryeworth Road
Charlton Kings
Cheltenham,
Gloucestershire, GL52 6LG
for all smocking supplies

Newey Goodman
Sedgley Road
West Tipton
West Midlands
DY4 8AH
for sewing equipment

United States

Aardvark Adventures
PO Box 2449
Livermore, CA94551
for fabrics, threads and trims

Herrschers
Hoover Road
Stevens Point, WI 54481
for general tools and equipment

Nancy's Notions
PO Box 683
Dept 32, Beave Dam
WI 53916
*for sewing, quilting, beadwork,
appliqué and embroidery*

Australia

Coats Patons Crafts Pty Ltd
89–91 Peters Avenue
Mulgrave
VIC 3170

DMC Needlecraft Pty Ltd
51–55 Carrington Road
Marrickville
NSW 2204

Simply Stitches
153 Victoria Avenue
Chatswood
NSW 2067

Canada

Dressew
337 W Hastings Street
Vancouver, BC

ACKNOWLEDGEMENTS

The publisher would like to thank the talented stitchers who generously loaned their work for inclusion in this publication:
Sarah Campbell for the felt hat, p.28; Hilary Hollingworth, p.65;
Shelagh Jarvis, pp.56–7 (based on a workshop with Jenny Rayment); Kath Poxon, p.121; Chris Slade, p.64.

Many thanks to the following people for stitching the many samples that appear in this publication: Sue Copeman, Barbara Lethbridge,
Joyce Mallinson, Brenda Monk, Lynn Simms, Barbara Smith, Adele and Hayley Wainwright, and Rita Whitehorn.

Thanks also to the following companies for assisting with photography for this book: Bogod Machine Company for the loan of the sewing machine;
Bradshaw & Bradshaw, and Derby House for loaning fabric; Simplicity Ltd for the loan of the jacket on pp.7 and 29, the bridesmaid's dress
on pp.27 and 29, the evening gown on p.30, the velour top on p.61, the velvet jacket and trousers on p.70, and the child's outfit on p.79.